AF539291

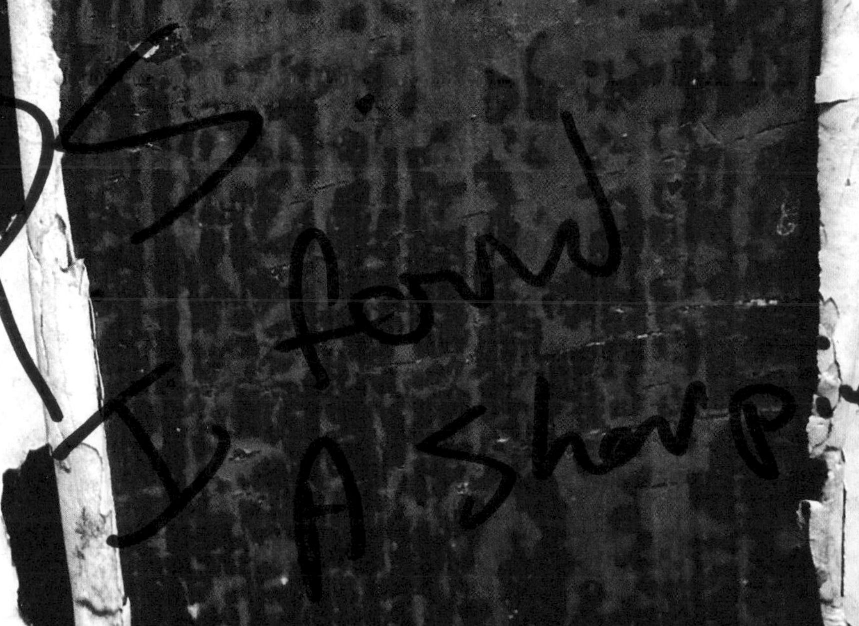
PS
I found
A Sharpie

Poster Boy
THE WAR OF ART

MARK BATTY PUBLISHER
NEW YORK CITY

The enemy has only images and illusions behind which he hides his true motives. Destroy the image and you break the enemy.

—Shaolin Abbot, *Enter the Dragon*

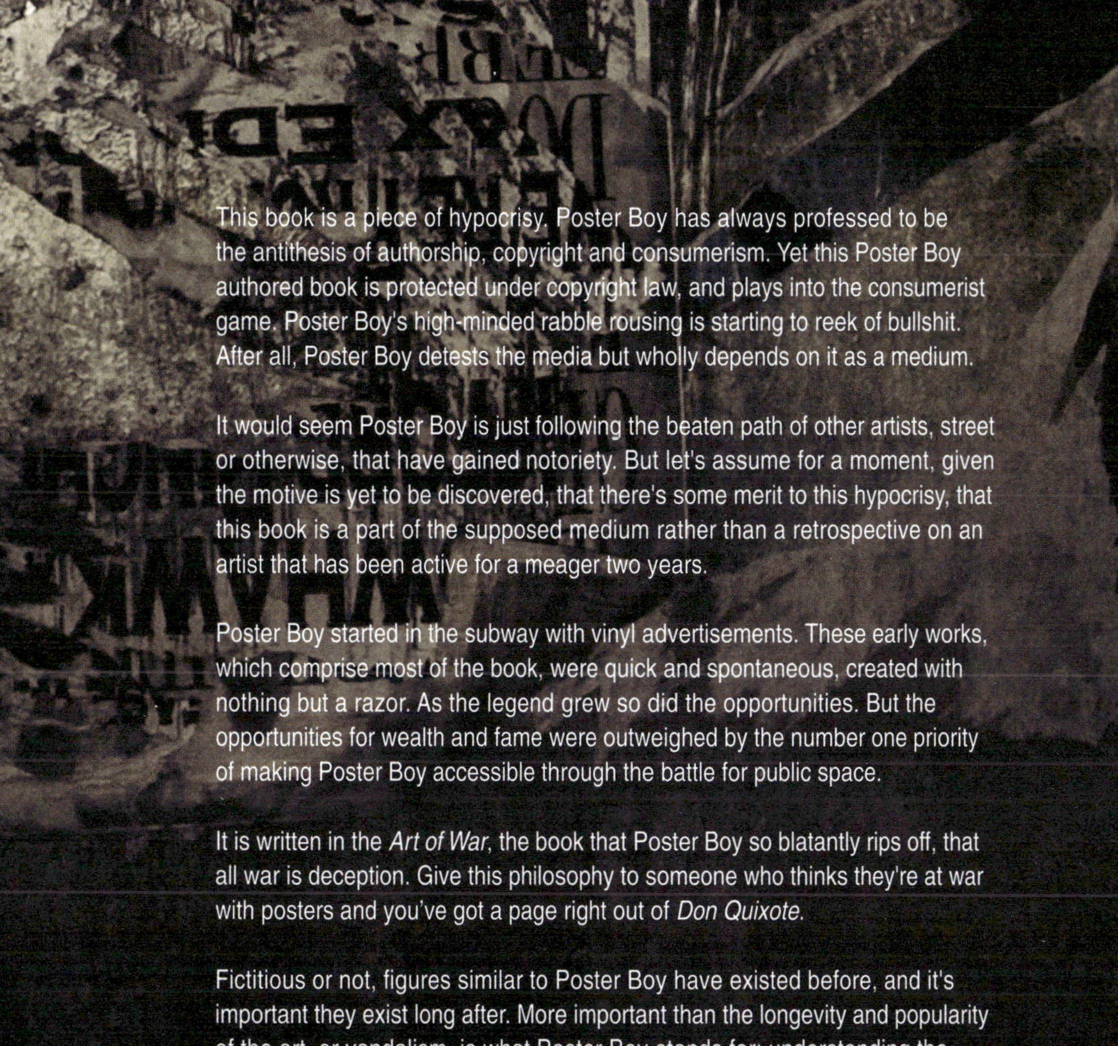

This book is a piece of hypocrisy. Poster Boy has always professed to be the antithesis of authorship, copyright and consumerism. Yet this Poster Boy authored book is protected under copyright law, and plays into the consumerist game. Poster Boy's high-minded rabble rousing is starting to reek of bullshit. After all, Poster Boy detests the media but wholly depends on it as a medium.

It would seem Poster Boy is just following the beaten path of other artists, street or otherwise, that have gained notoriety. But let's assume for a moment, given the motive is yet to be discovered, that there's some merit to this hypocrisy, that this book is a part of the supposed medium rather than a retrospective on an artist that has been active for a meager two years.

Poster Boy started in the subway with vinyl advertisements. These early works, which comprise most of the book, were quick and spontaneous, created with nothing but a razor. As the legend grew so did the opportunities. But the opportunities for wealth and fame were outweighed by the number one priority of making Poster Boy accessible through the battle for public space.

It is written in the *Art of War*, the book that Poster Boy so blatantly rips off, that all war is deception. Give this philosophy to someone who thinks they're at war with posters and you've got a page right out of *Don Quixote.*

Fictitious or not, figures similar to Poster Boy have existed before, and it's important they exist long after. More important than the longevity and popularity of the art, or vandalism, is what Poster Boy stands for: understanding the difference between what is legal and what is right.

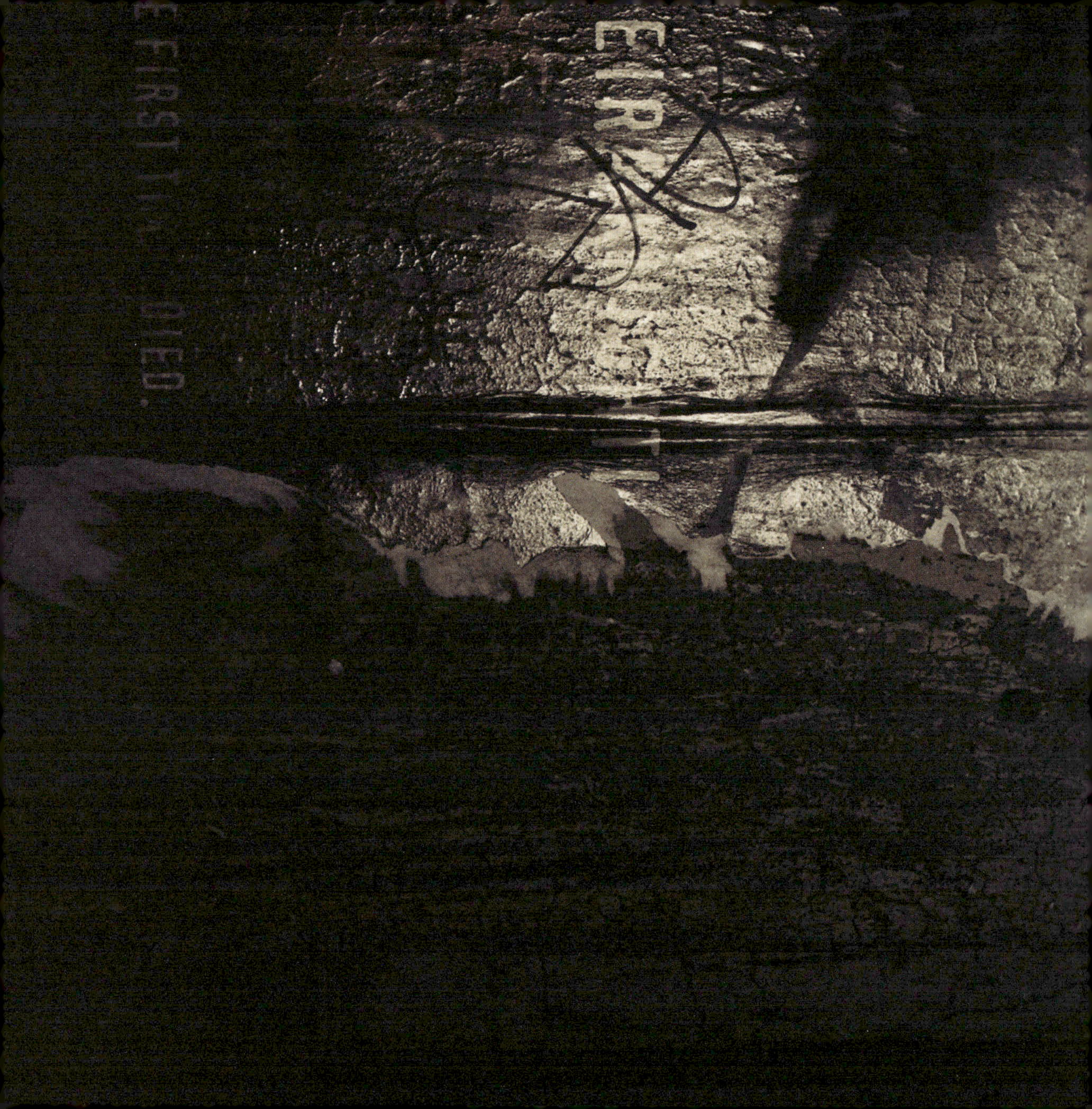

TABLE OF CONTENTS

WORKS ON VINYL

ABETMENTS

EXHIBITIONS

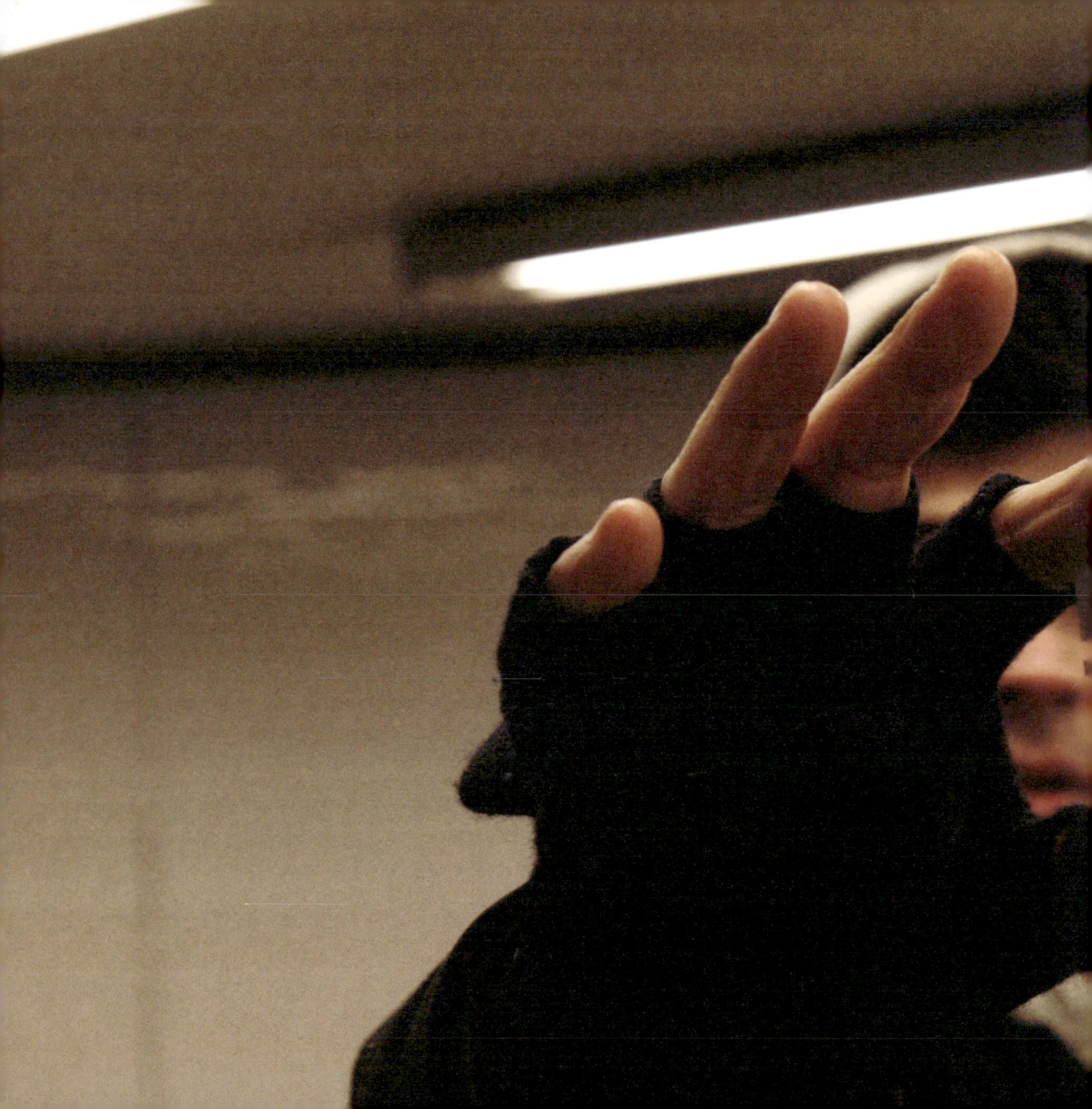

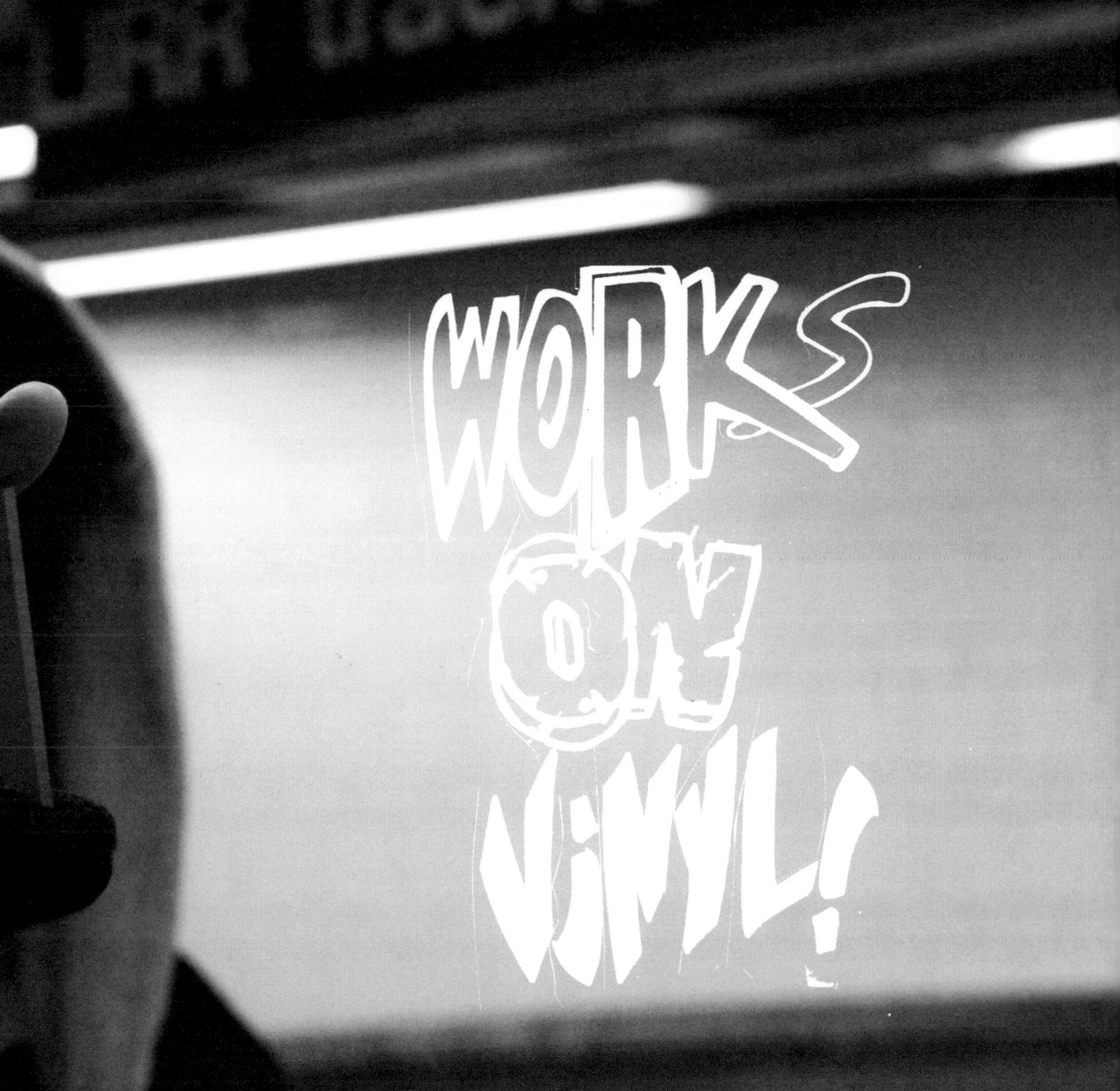
WORKS
ON
VINYL!

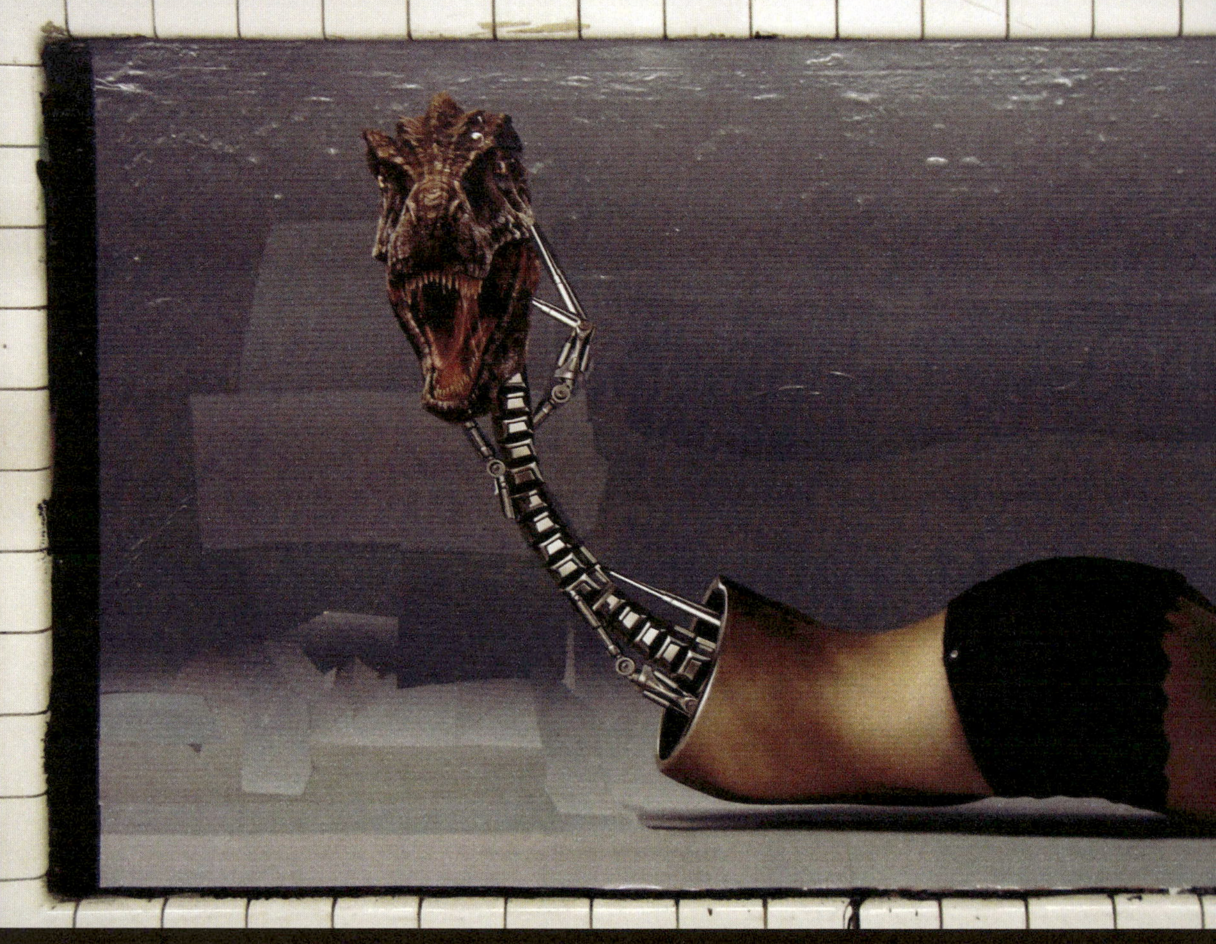

BACK TO THE FUTURE The new sci-fi made retro…again.

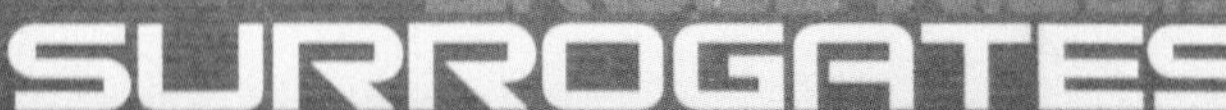
HUMAN PERFECTION. WHAT COULD GO WRONG?
$5.85
BRUCE WILLIS
SURROGATES

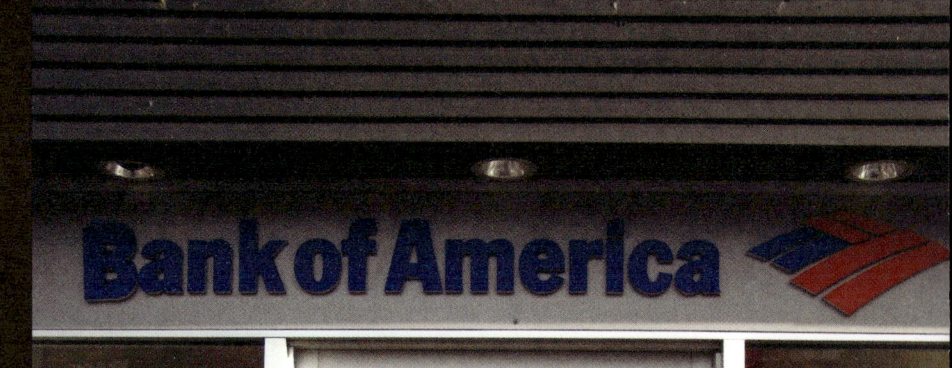

BANK OF AMERICA / BAILOUT

Between sub-prime mortgages and bailouts for Wall Street and banks, America's moral economy has been bankrupt for a while now.

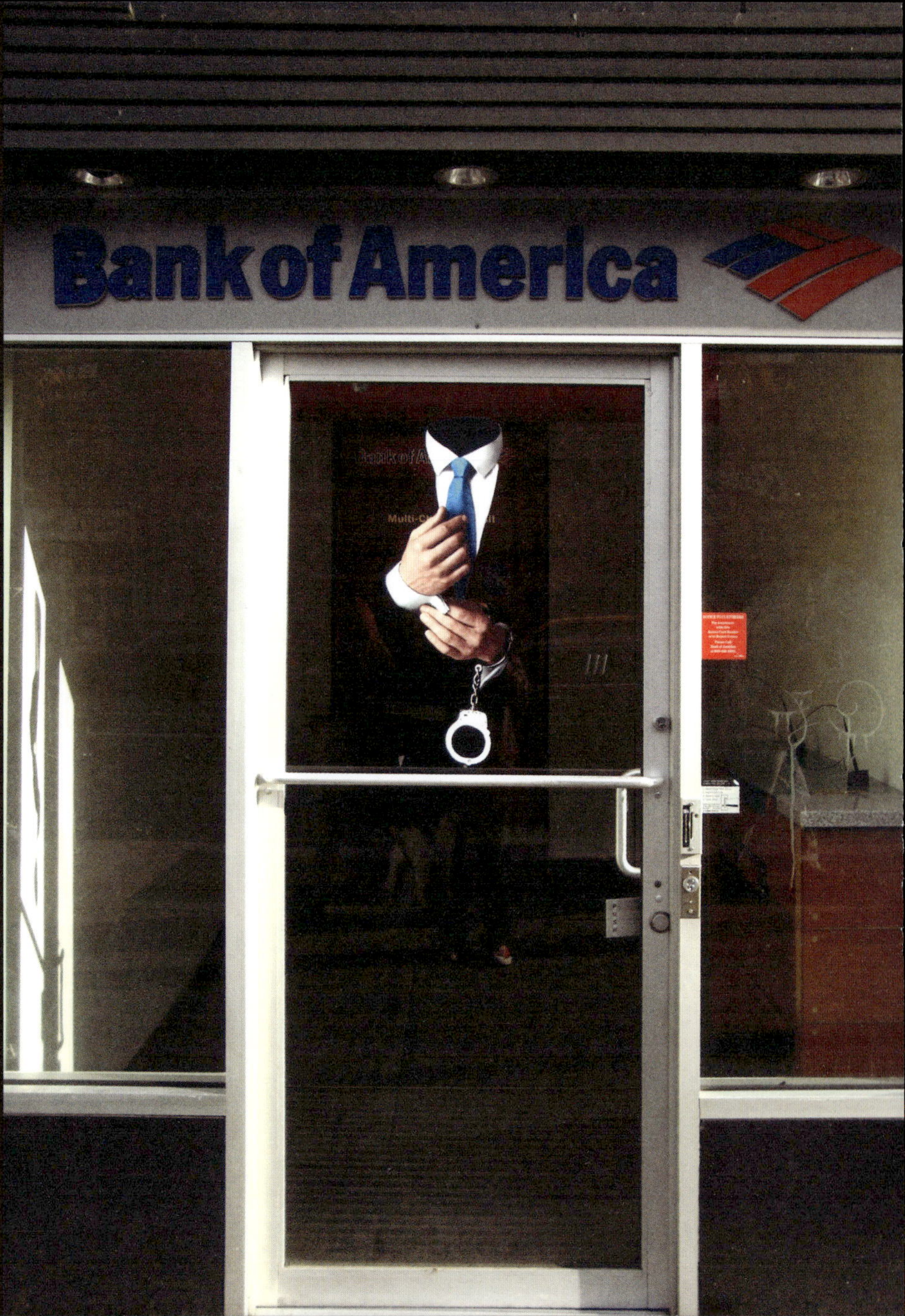

BAILO♥T

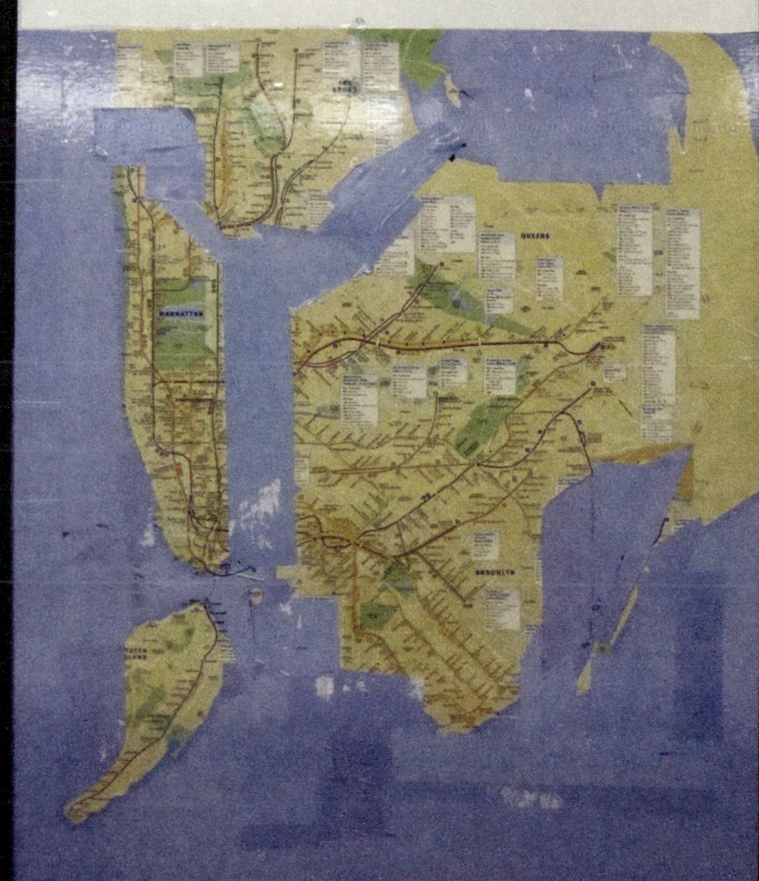

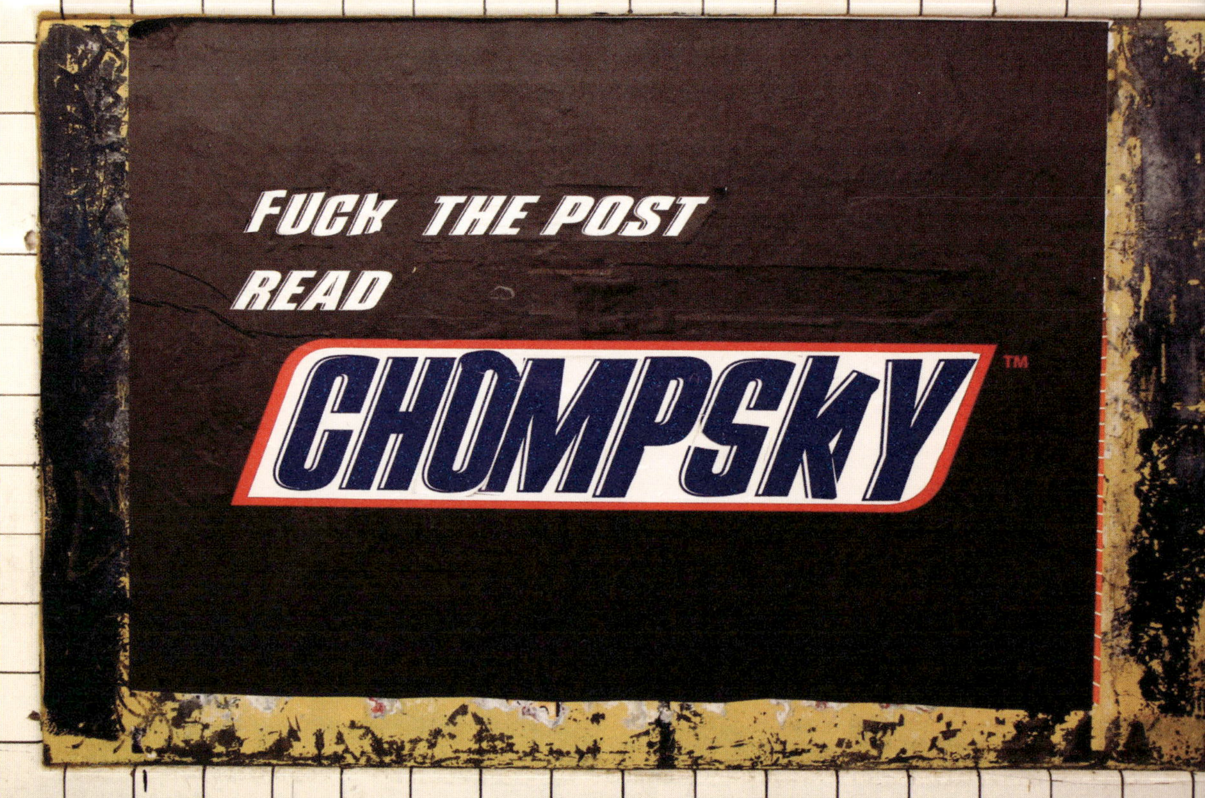
WILLOUGHBY
FUCK THE POST
READ
CHOMPSKY™

INVEST IN SOME HIGH-YIELD

MUCHEWAL FUNDS™

READ THE POST ON YOUR

CHEWNMUTE™

READ CHOMPSKY

This ad campaign's play on words is moderately clever and ultimately annoying. The "P" in Chompsky isn't necessarily groundbreaking either, but it sure beats anything the *Post* puts out.

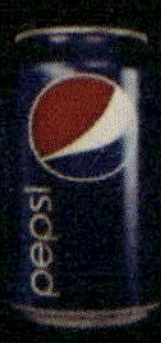

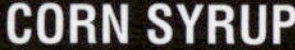

CORN SYRUP

Stating the obvious about soda isn't hard. Creating a freehand font is.

DAY OF TREASON

An Adam Sandler movie finally serves a purpose.

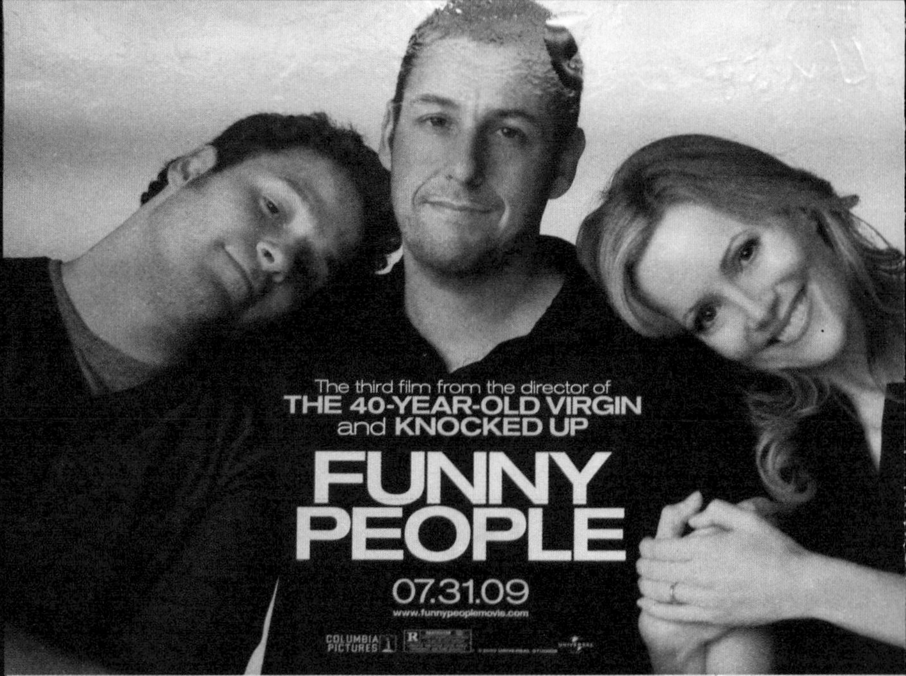

The third film from the director of
THE 40-YEAR-OLD VIRGIN
and KNOCKED UP
FUNNY
PEOPLE
07.31.09
www.funnypeoplemovie.com

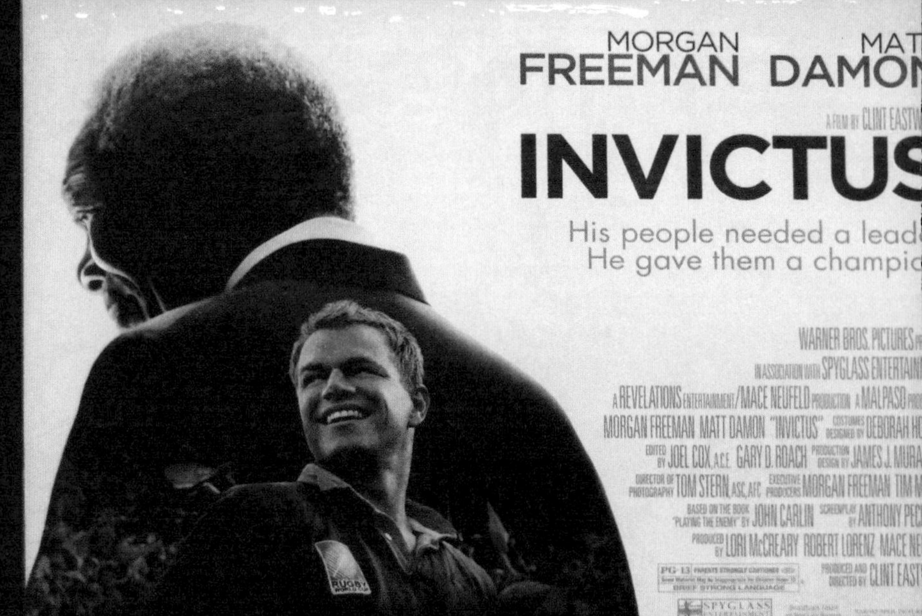

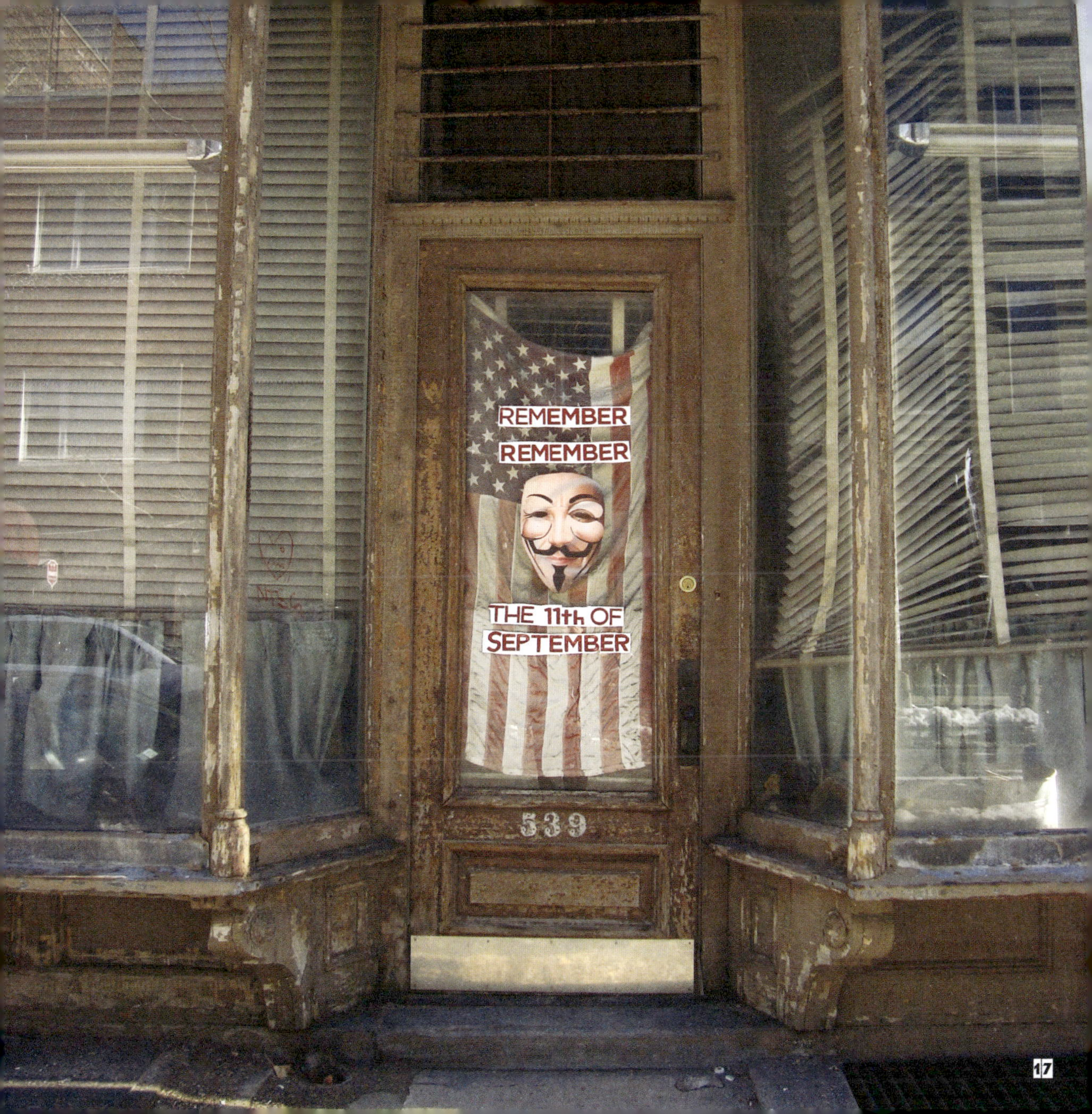
REMEMBER
REMEMBER
THE 11th OF
SEPTEMBER
539

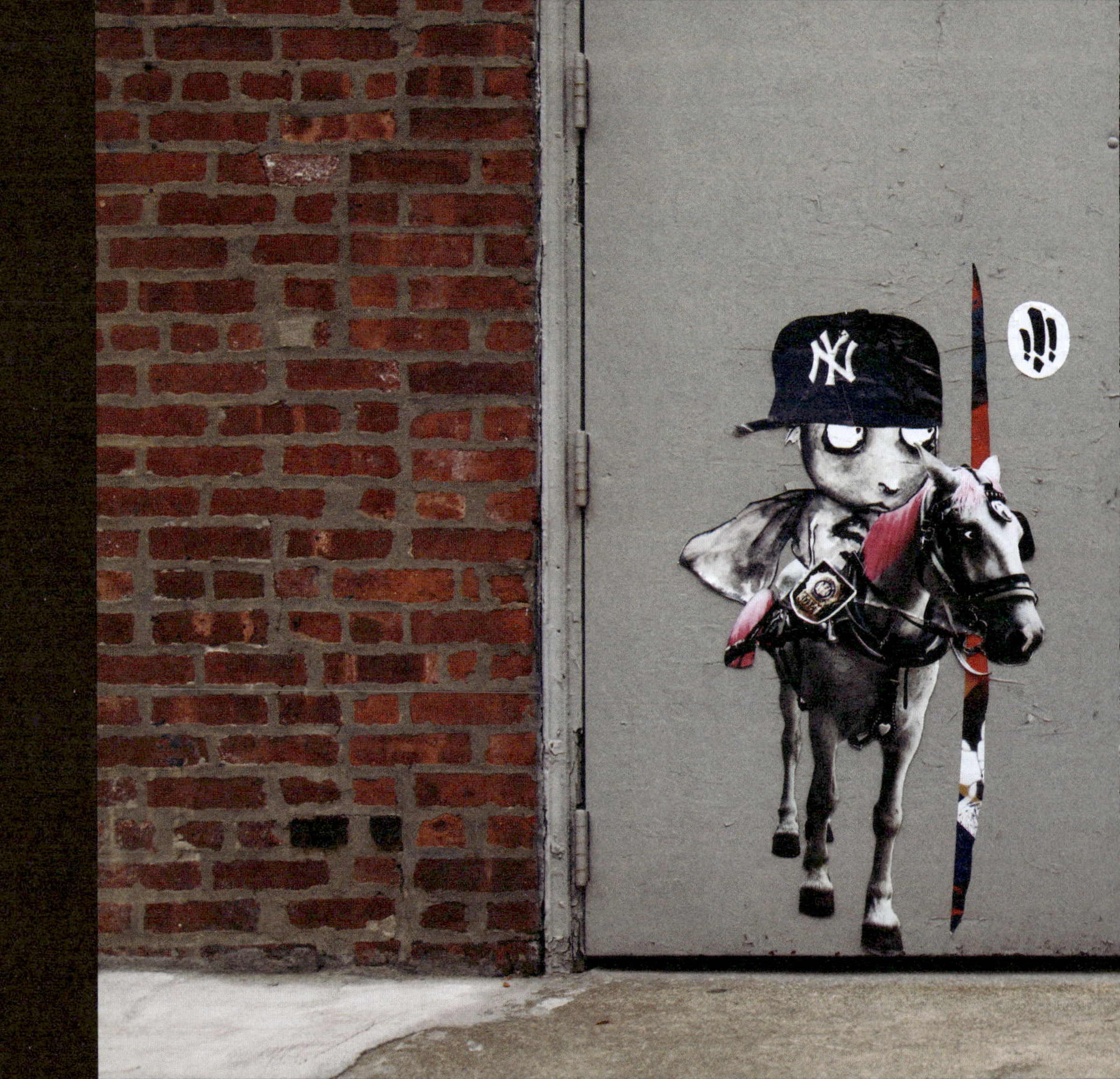
NY

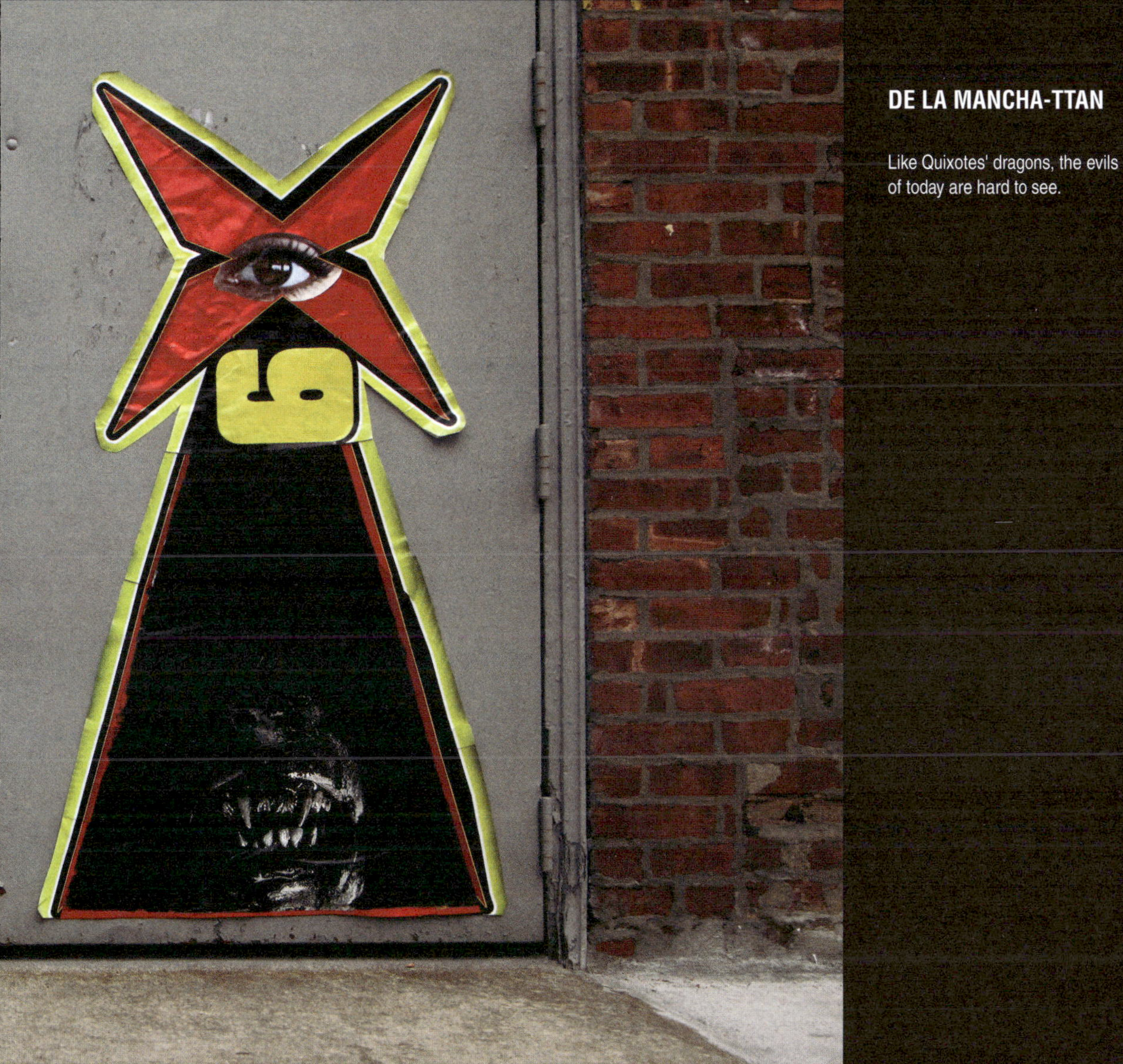

DE LA MANCHA-TTAN

Like Quixotes' dragons, the evils of today are hard to see.

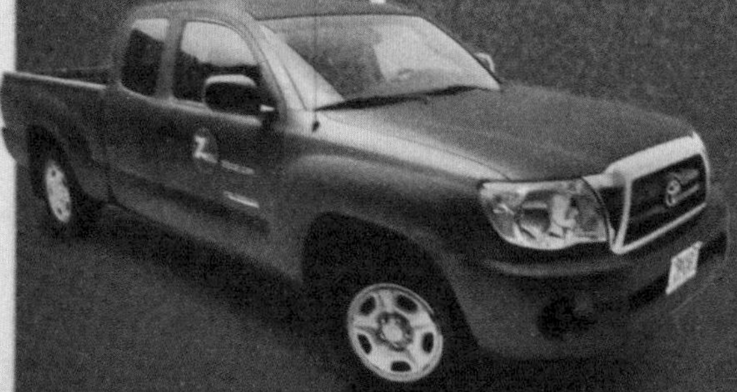

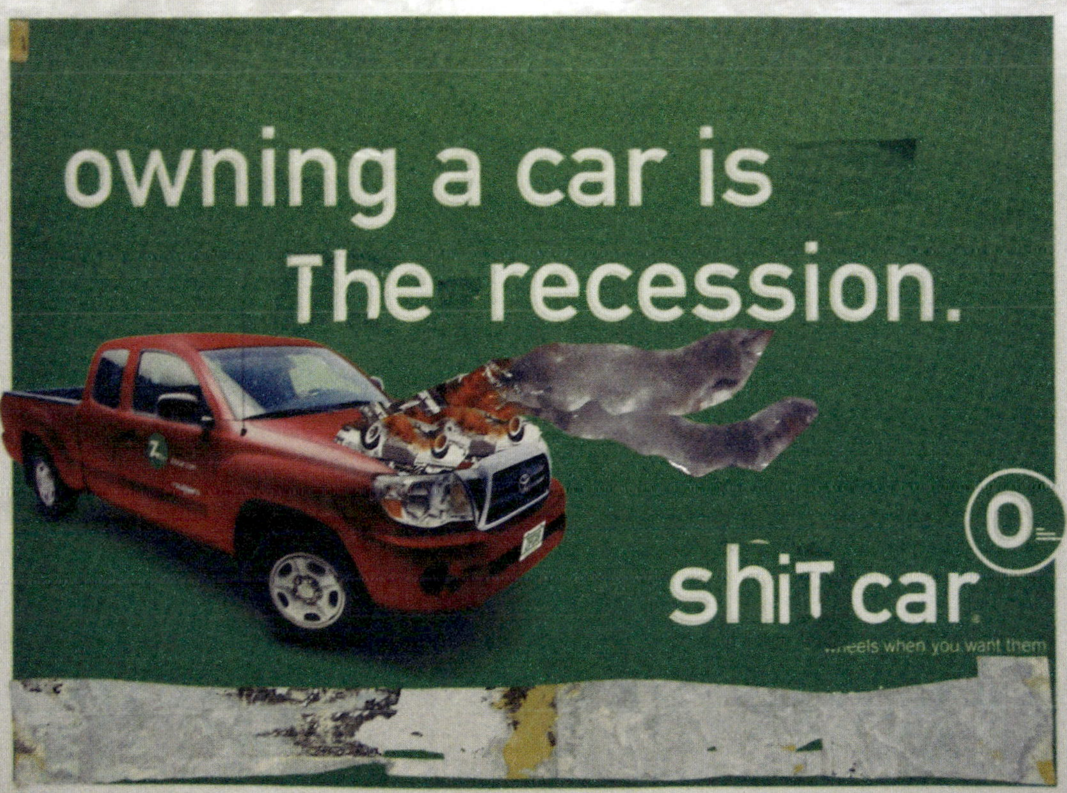

DIAGNOSIS

The auto industry may not be solely
responsible for the economy's dis-

FAT CHANCE

Lies and the liars that tell them: neither drinking nor dancing will cure gluttony.

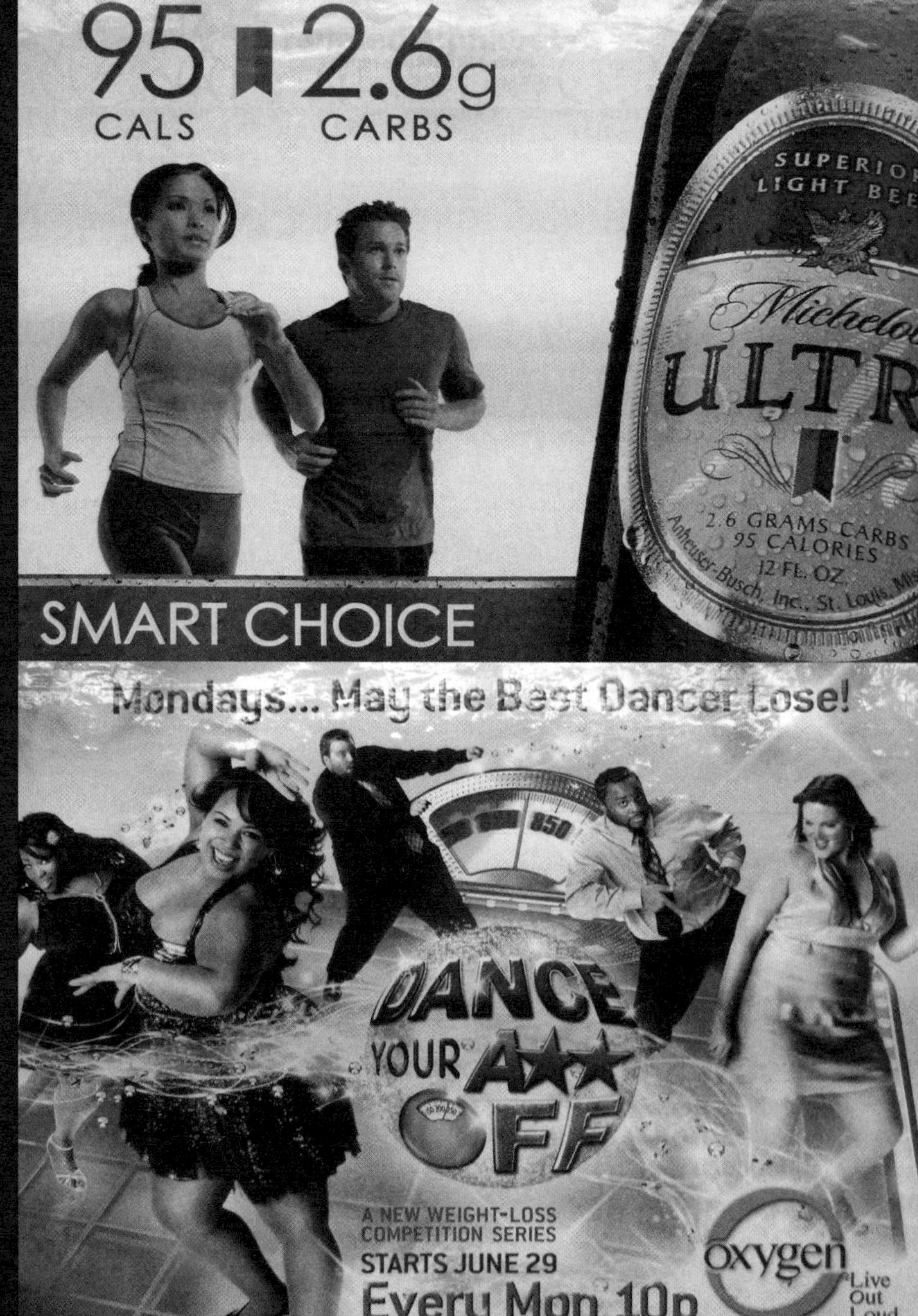

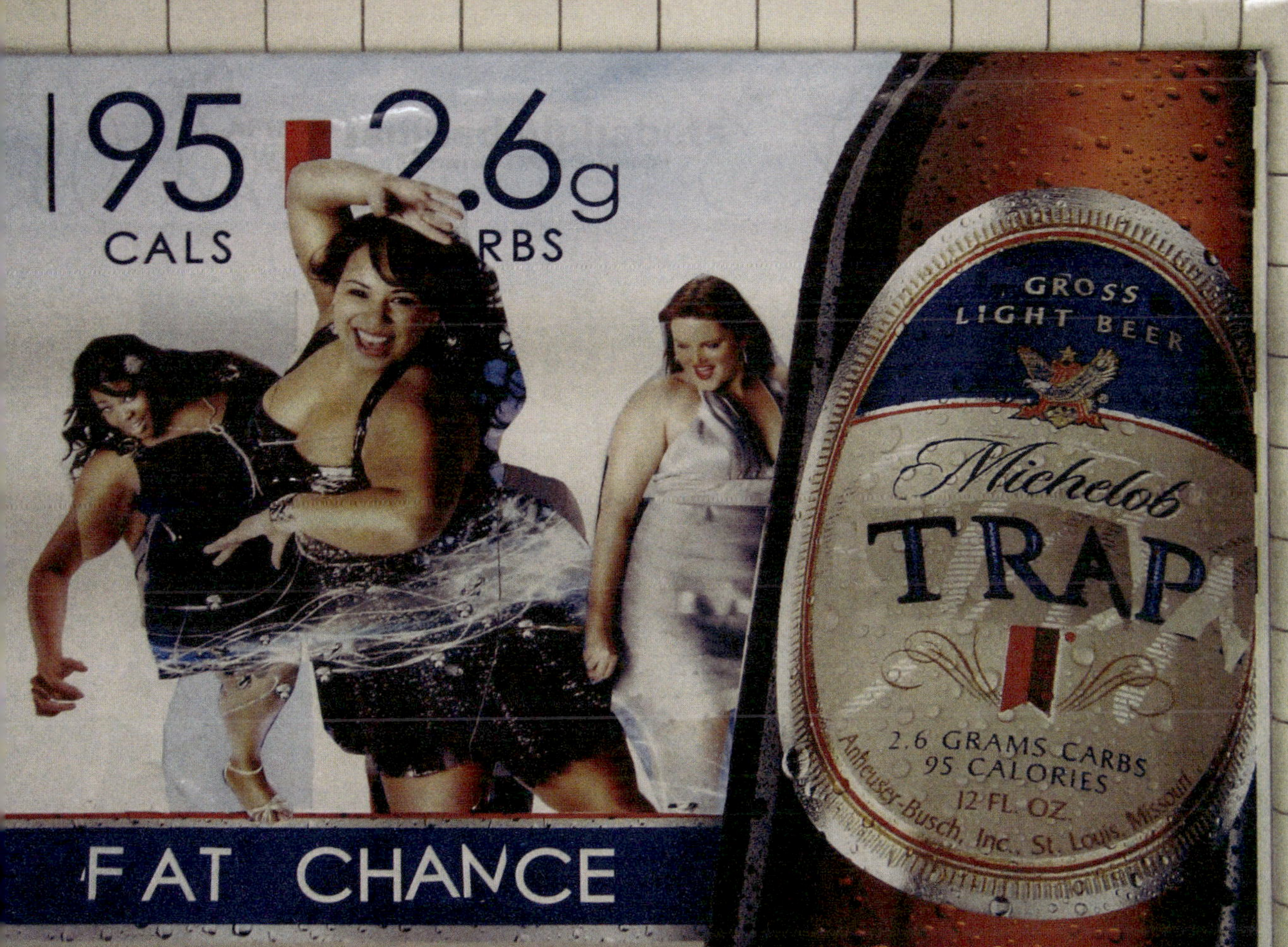

195
CALS
2.6g
RBS
GROSS LIGHT BEER
Michelob
TRAP
2.6 GRAMS CARBS
95 CALORIES
12 FL. OZ.
Anheuser-Busch, Inc., St. Louis, Missouri
FAT CHANCE

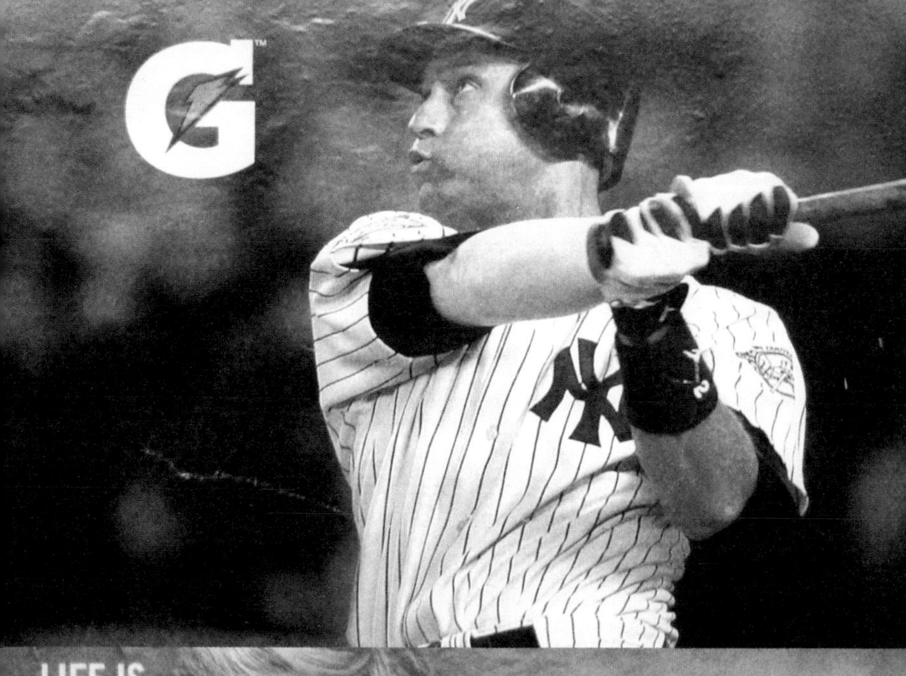

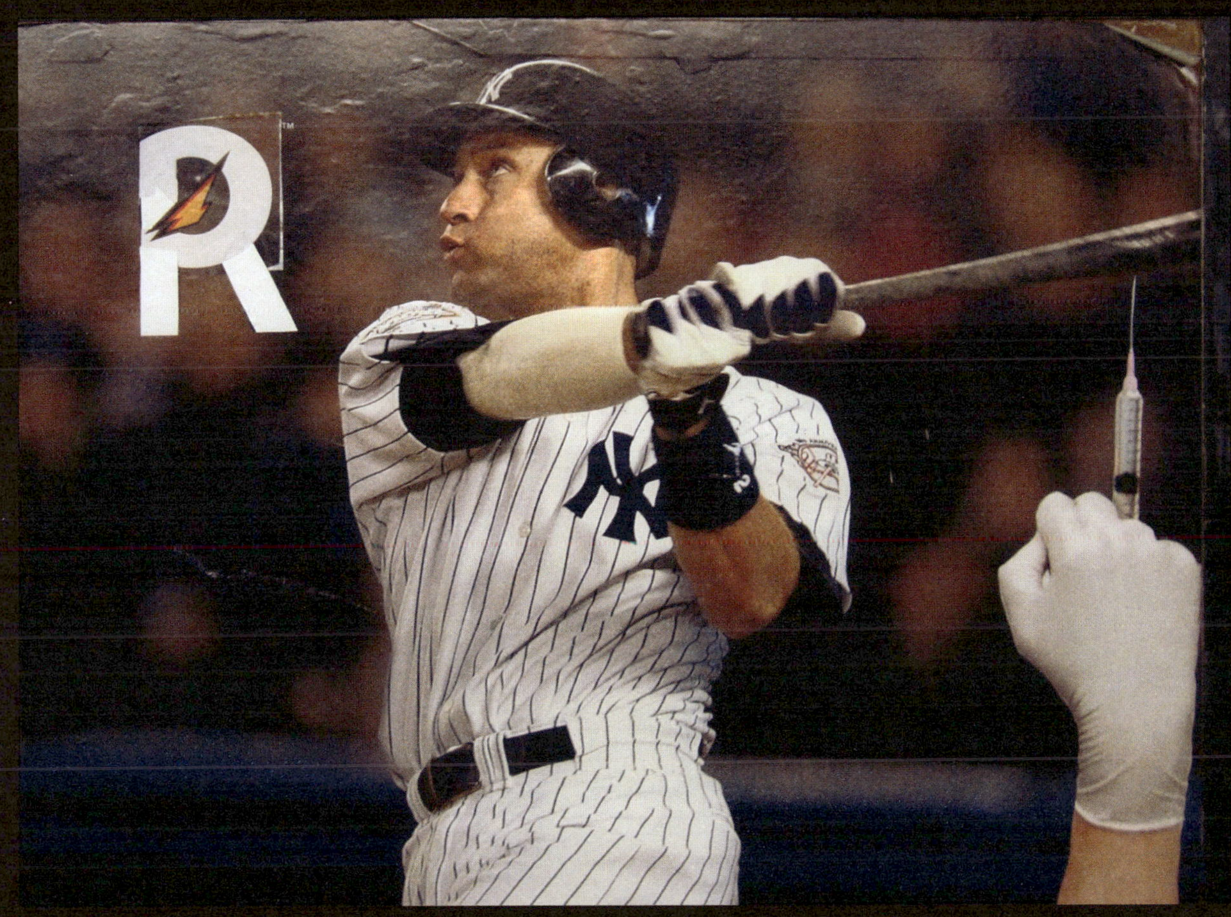

GATOROIDS

Forget the front line. The real biological war is being fought on television.

IRONY OF THE NEGRO POLICEMAN

After Officer Omar Edwards was shot dead in Harlem by fellow officers Jean-Michel Basquiat's, "Irony of the Negro Policeman," immediately came to mind. The only thing left was to find the posters that would help make that connection.

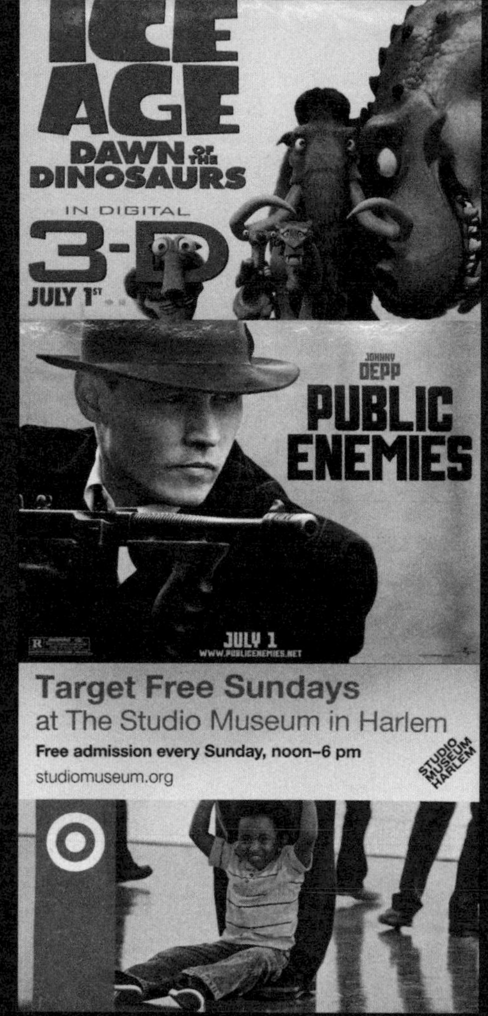

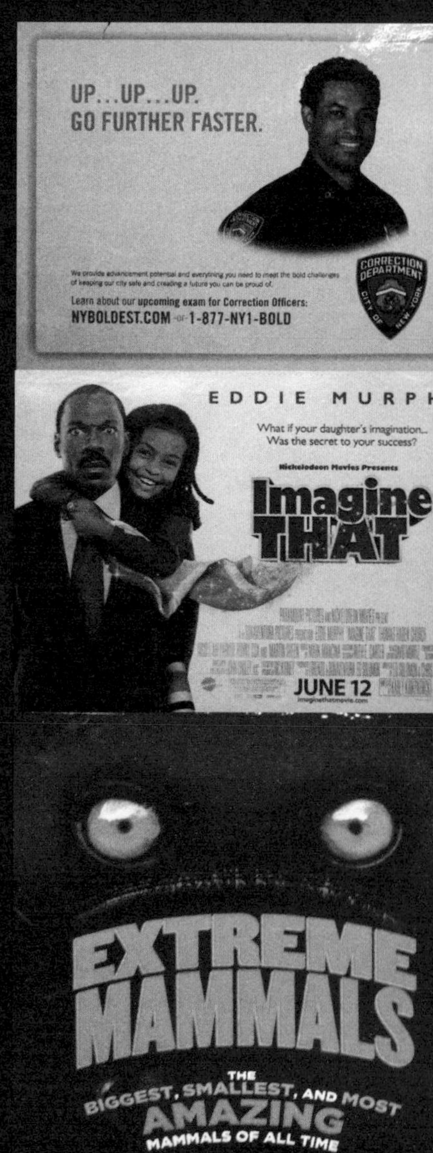

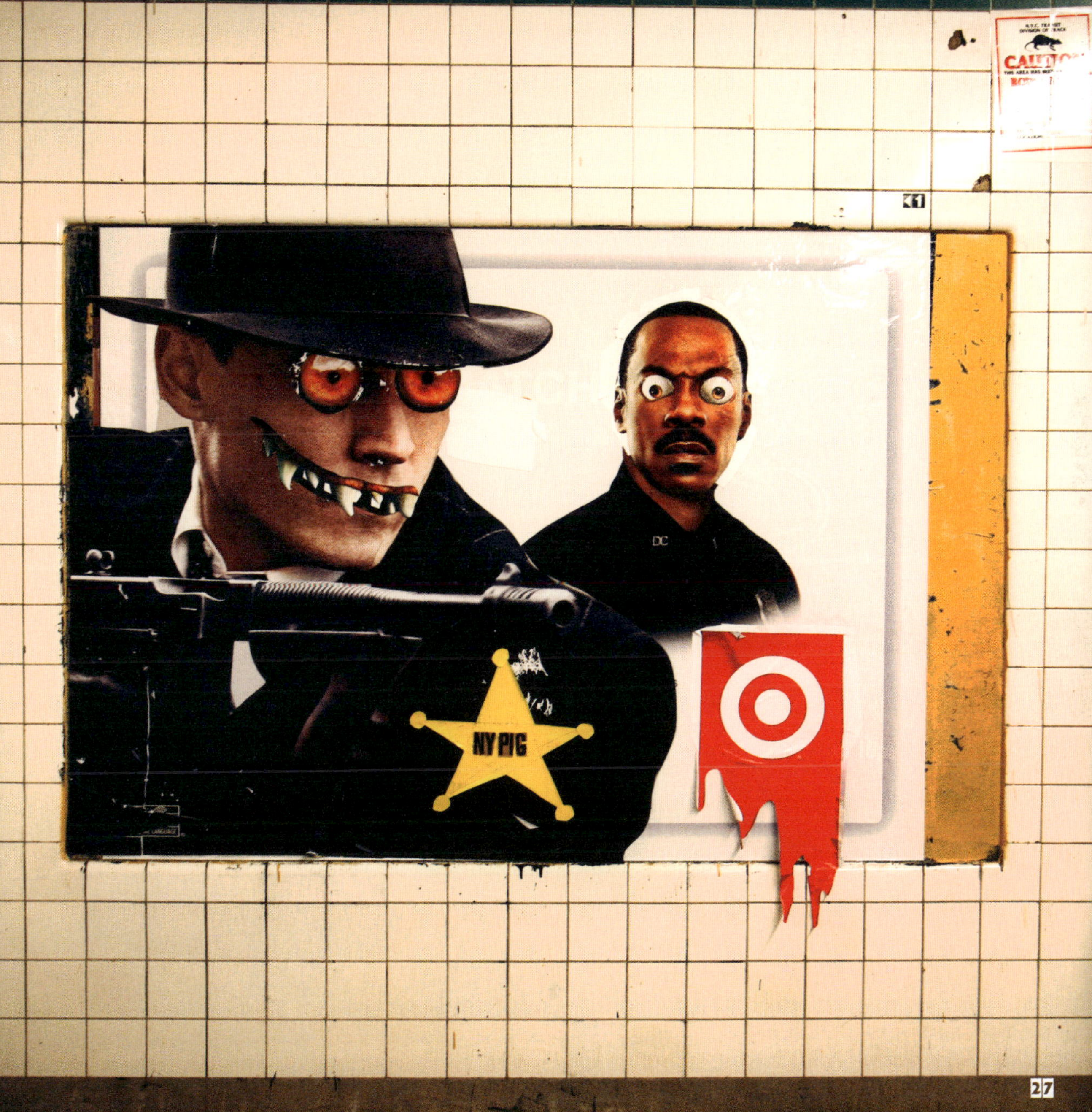

CAUTION
NY PIG
DC

1

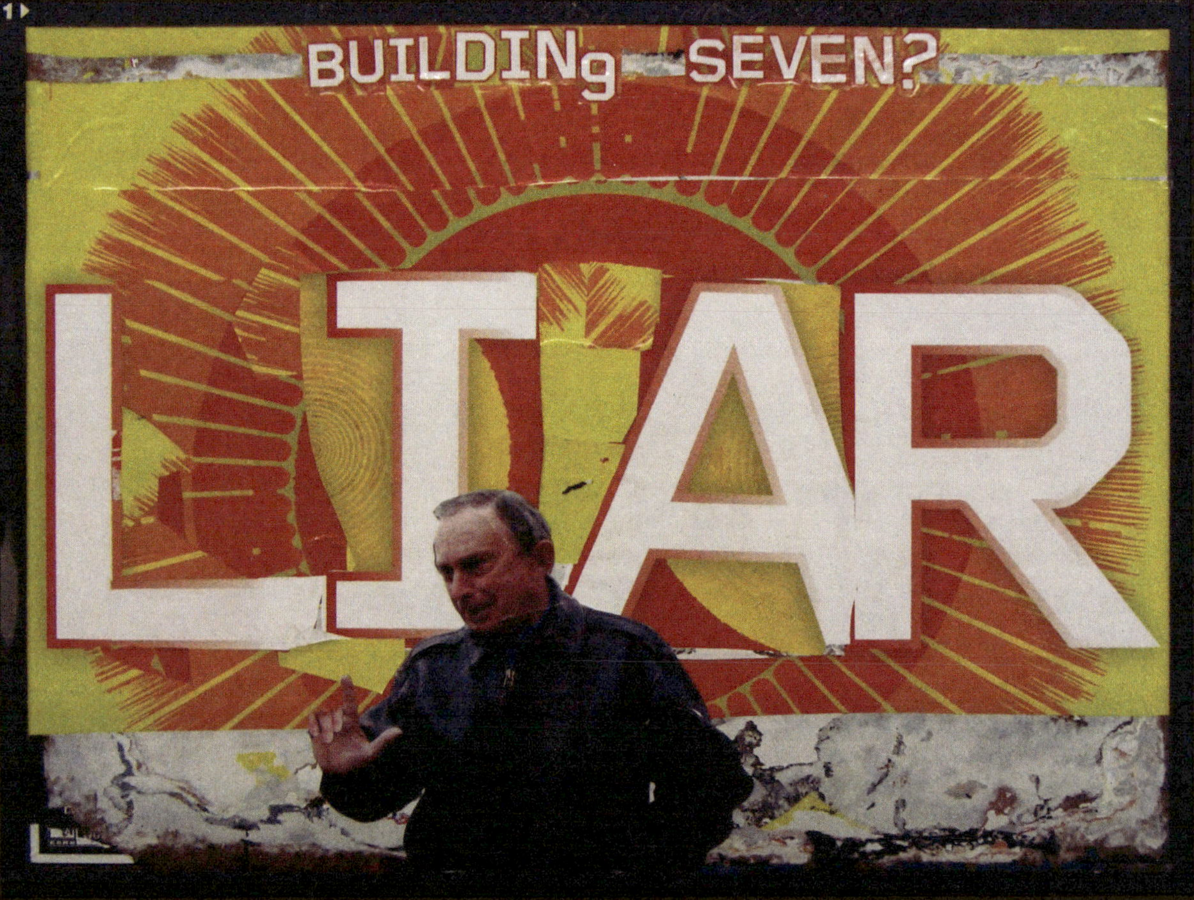

BUILDINg SEVEN?

LIAR

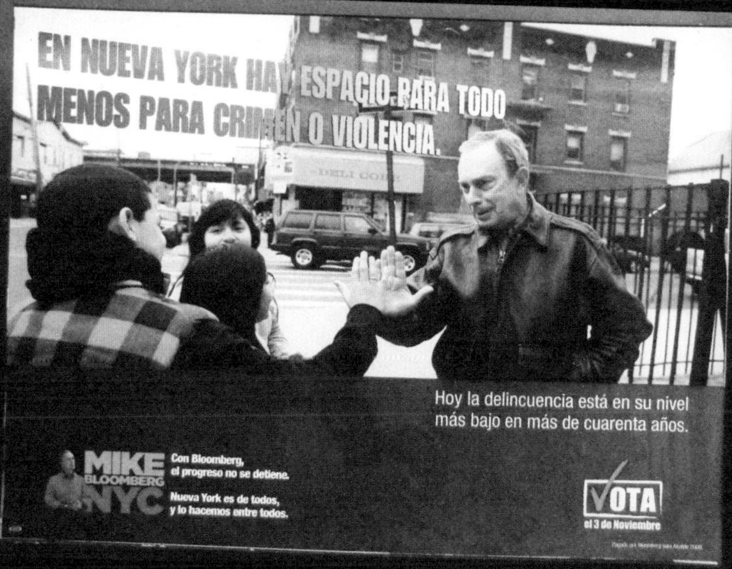

WINNER! 2009 TONY AWARD
BEST MUSICAL REVIVAL

HAIR

TELECHARGE.COM OR 212-239-6200 · AL HIRSCHFELD THEATRE, 302 W 45TH ST (BETWEEN 8TH & 9TH AVES) · HAIRBROADWAY.COM

LIAR

Al rey Mike le gusta aprendir el espanol. Mike está desnudo.

Eat your words.

Let Zagat Be Your Guide.
on ZAGAT.com | on your phone | on your bookshelf

ZAGAT®

Eat your turds,

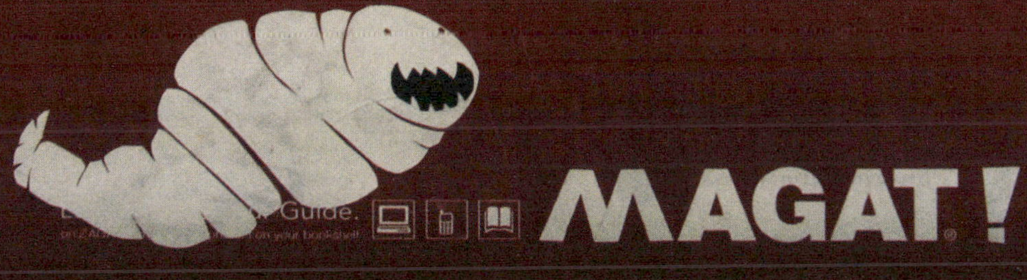

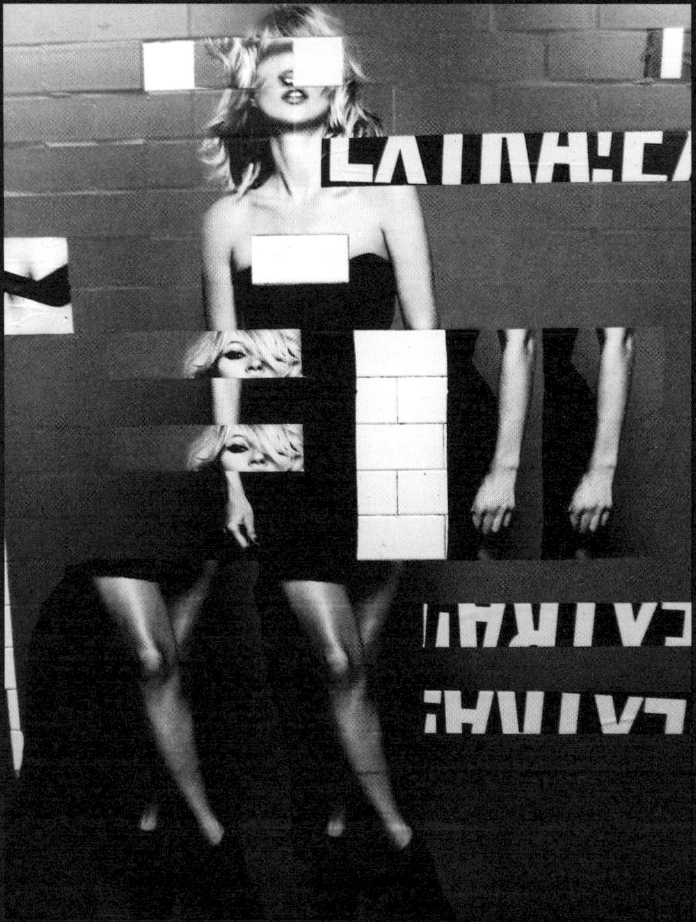

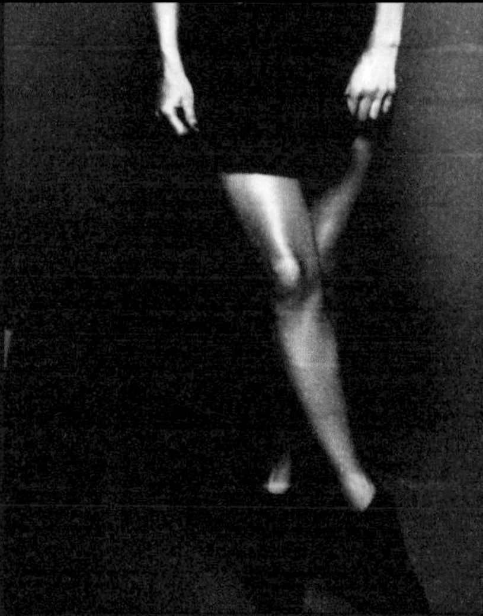

MOSSY TILES

The tiles are effective guidelines.

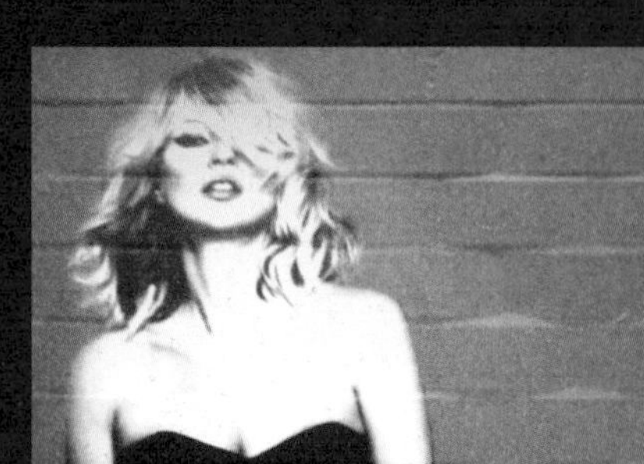

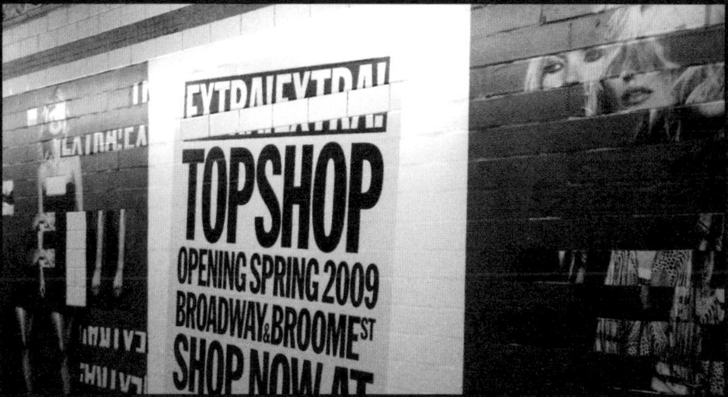

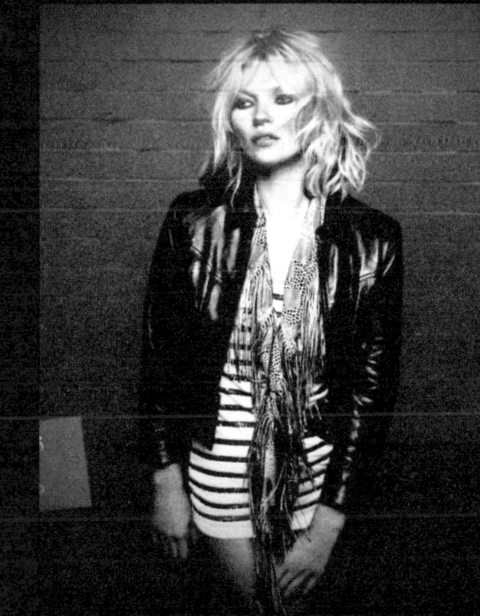

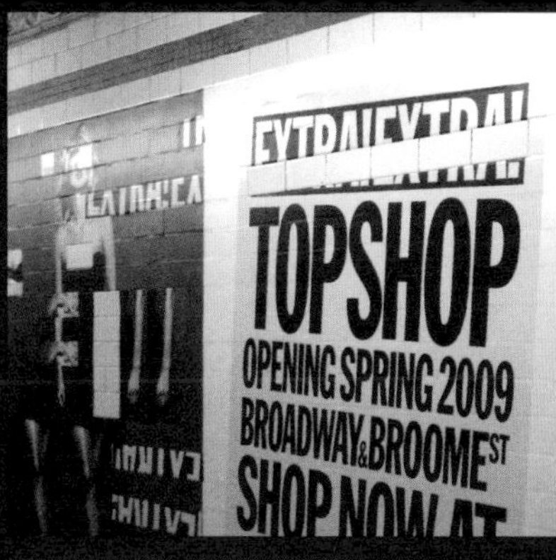
TOPSHOP
OPENING SPRING 2009
BROADWAY & BROOME ST
SHOP NOW AT

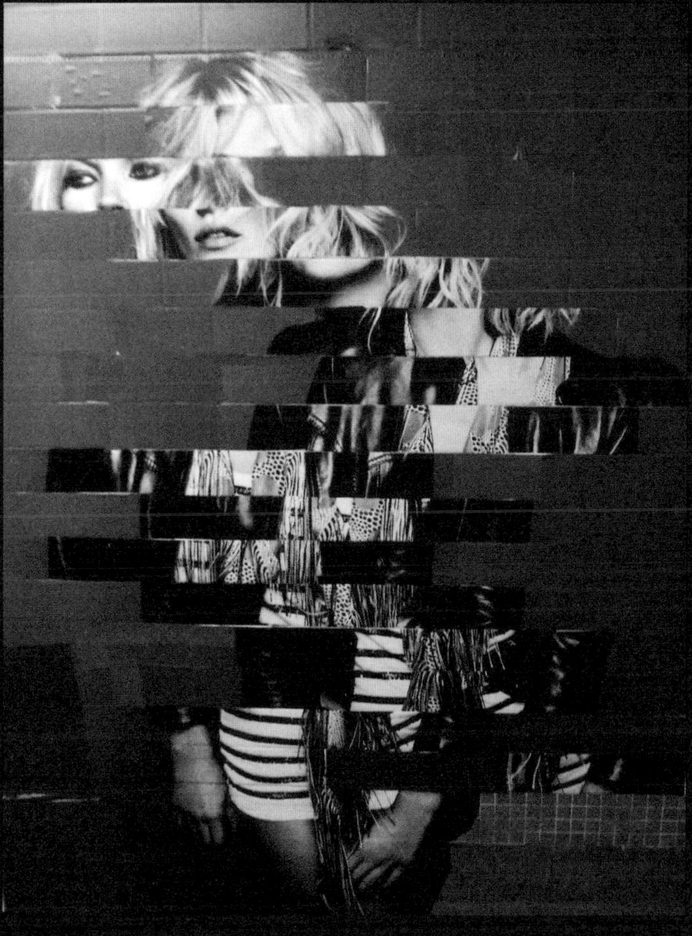

...NOT

By the time your artwork makes it onto one of these posters you've cooled down to tepid.

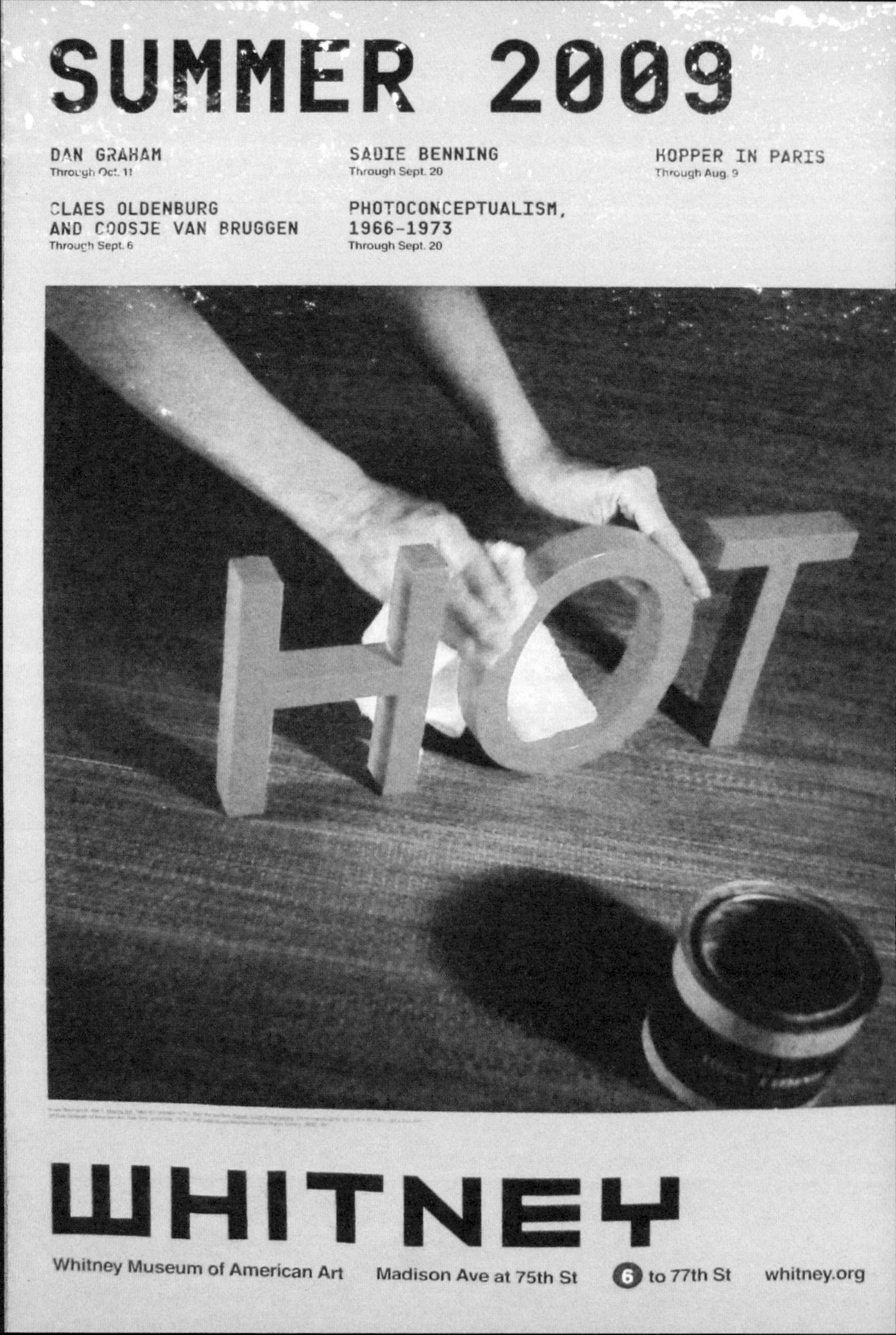

SUMMER 2009

DAN GRAHAM
Through Oct. 11

SADIE BENNING
Through Sept. 20

HOPPER IN PARIS
Through Aug. 9

CLAES OLDENBURG AND COOSJE VAN BRUGGEN
Through Sept. 6

PHOTOCONCEPTUALISM, 1966–1973
Through Sept. 20

HOT

WHITNEY

Whitney Museum of American Art Madison Ave at 75th St 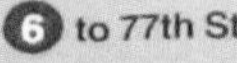 to 77th St whitney.org

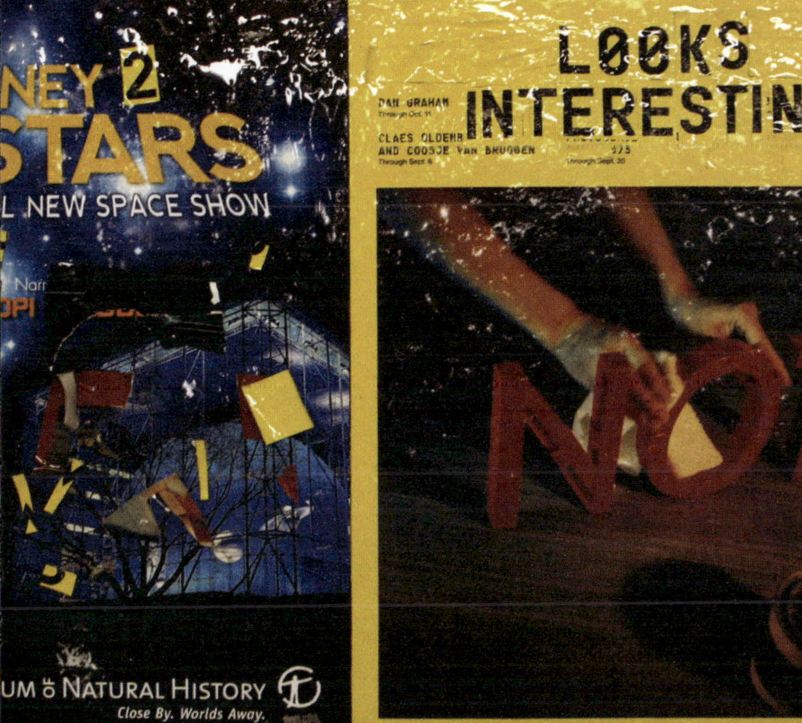
CARRO
NEY 2
STARS
L NEW SPACE SHOW
UM OF NATURAL HISTORY
Close By. Worlds Away.
NASA
L00KS
INTERESTINg...
DAN GRAHAM
Through Oct. 11
CLAES OLDENB
AND COOSJE VAN BRUGGEN
Through Sept. 6
NOT
SHITTY
Whitney Museum of American Art
Madison Ave at 75th St
6 to 77th St
whitney.org

REVENGE OF HOLOFERNES

Seeing the flailing arms in these jean ads brought to mind Artemisia Gentileschi's "Judith Beheading Holofernes."

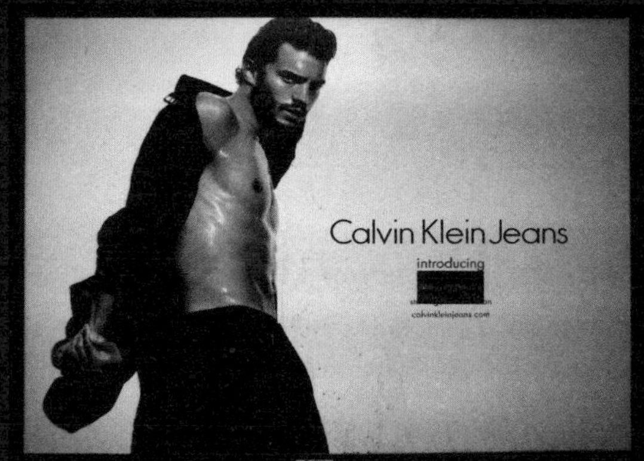

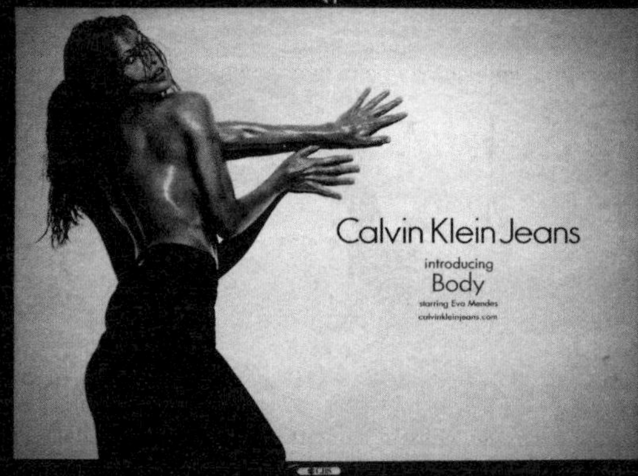

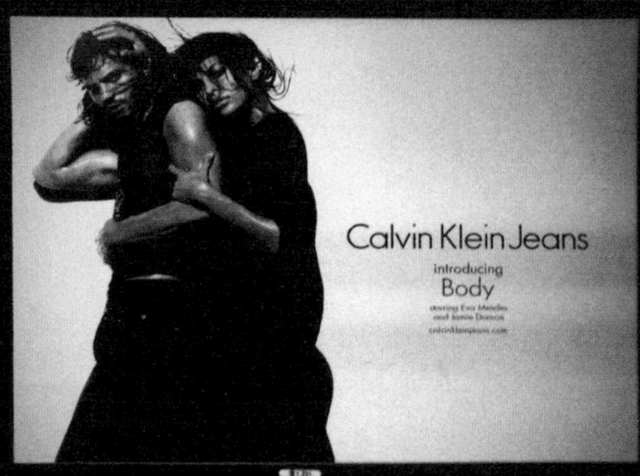

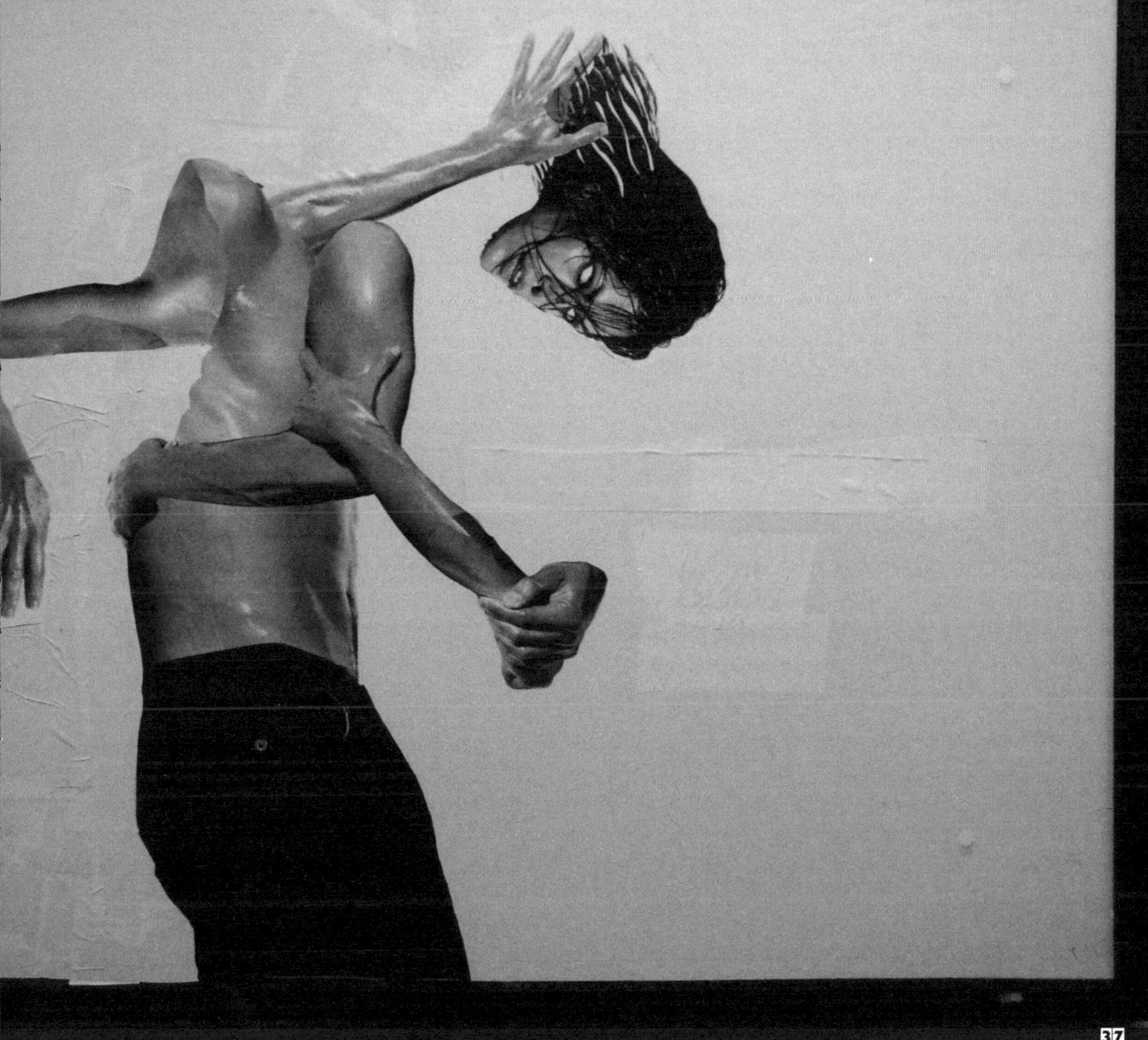

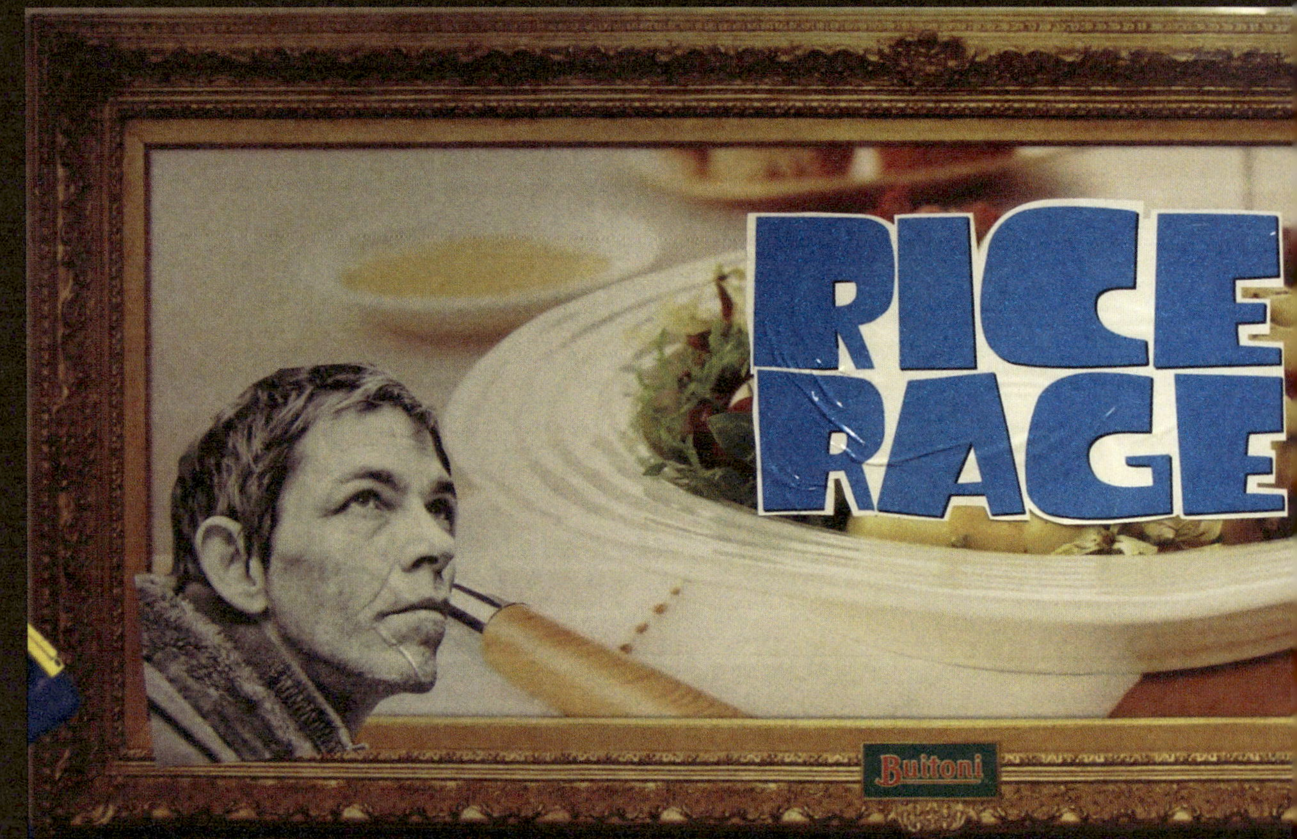

RICE RAGE

High levels of consumption in one place mean high levels of exploitation in another. Free trade in Haiti is a good example.

ICE AGE
DAWN OF THE DINOSAURS
IN DIGITAL
3-D
JULY 1ST

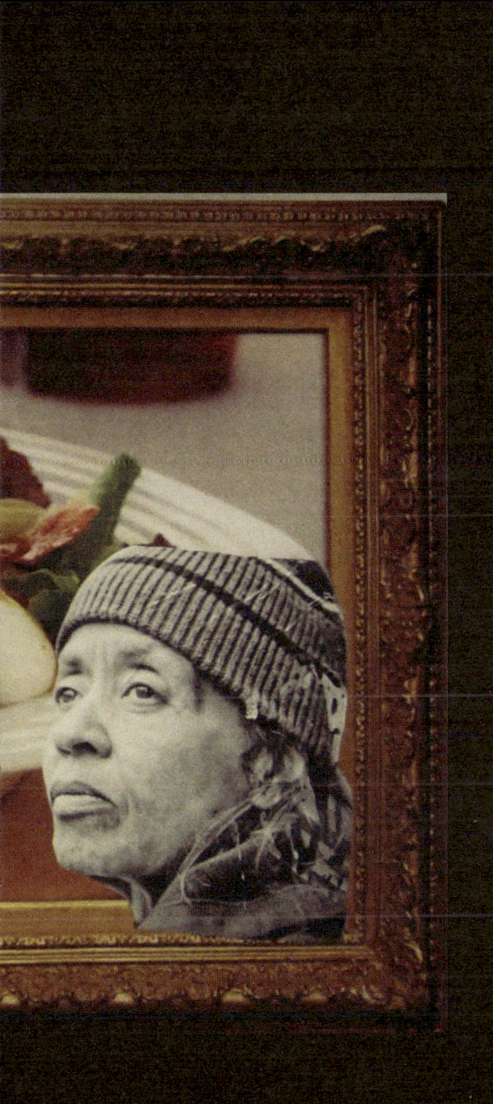

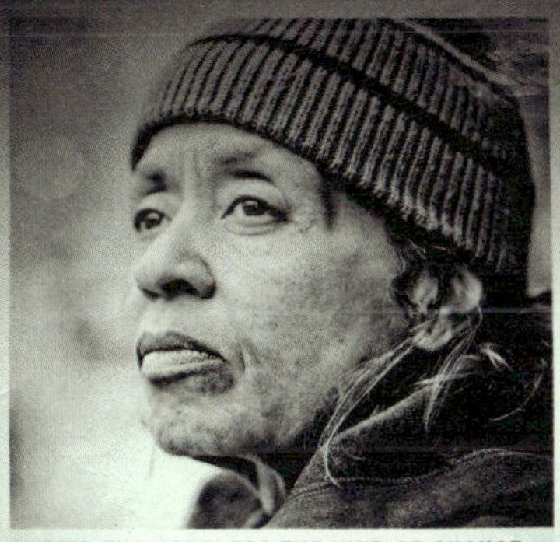
GIVE THE HOMELESS THE KIND OF CHANGE THEY CAN REALLY USE
Through the combined efforts of NYC Street to Home and MTA Connections Outreach Teams, now all New Yorkers can help provide real change to help end homelessness. Our professional outreach services will help the homeless off the streets and subways and into housing. Working together, we can give the homeless quarters of a different kind.
CALL 311
GIVE REAL CHANGE TO THE HOMELESS. CALL US AND WE'LL SEND AN OUTREACH TEAM TO HELP.

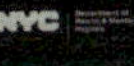
NYC

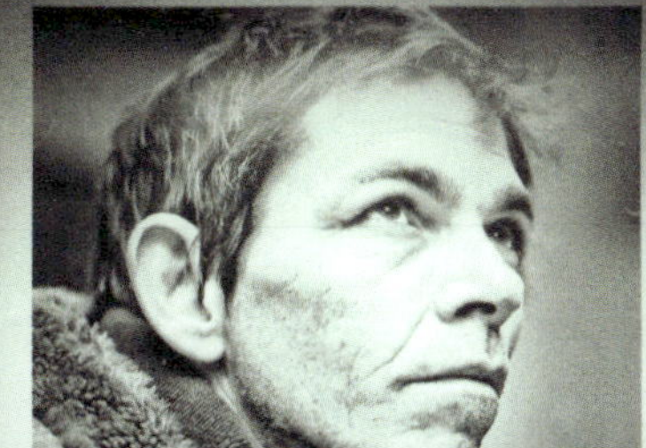

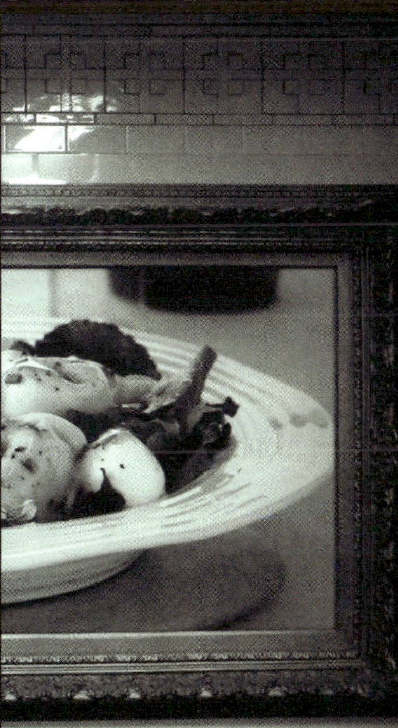

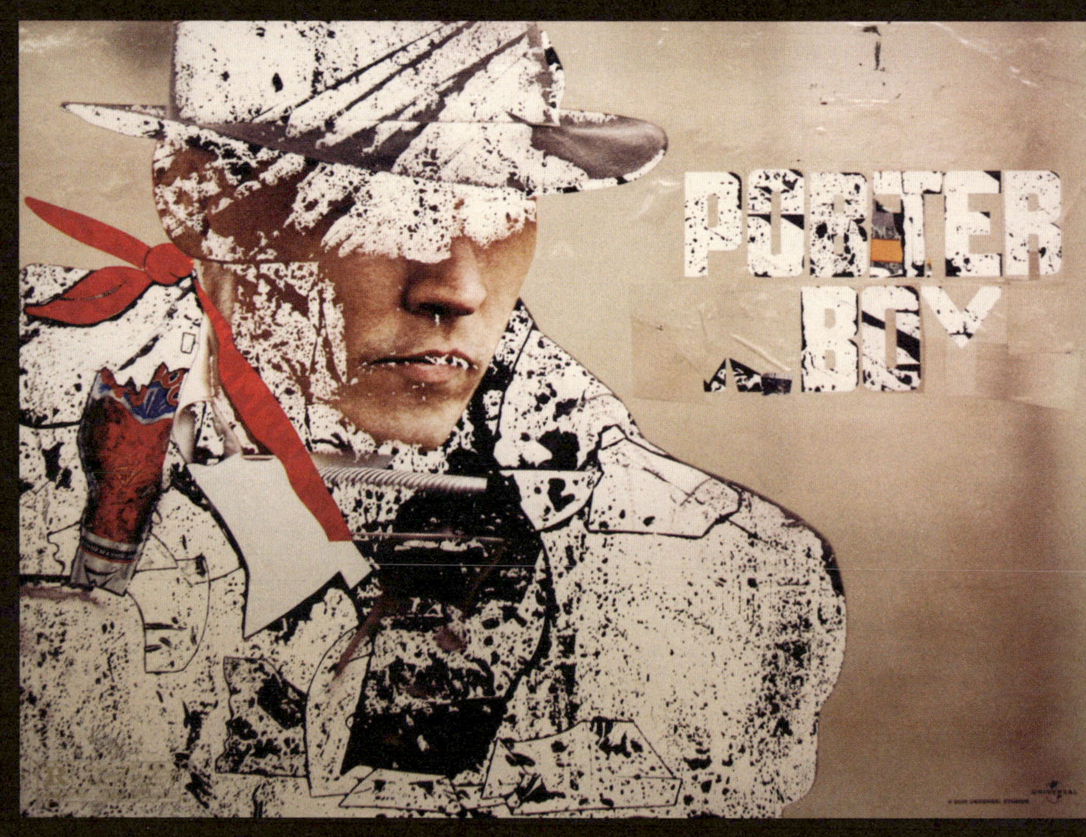
POSTER
BOY

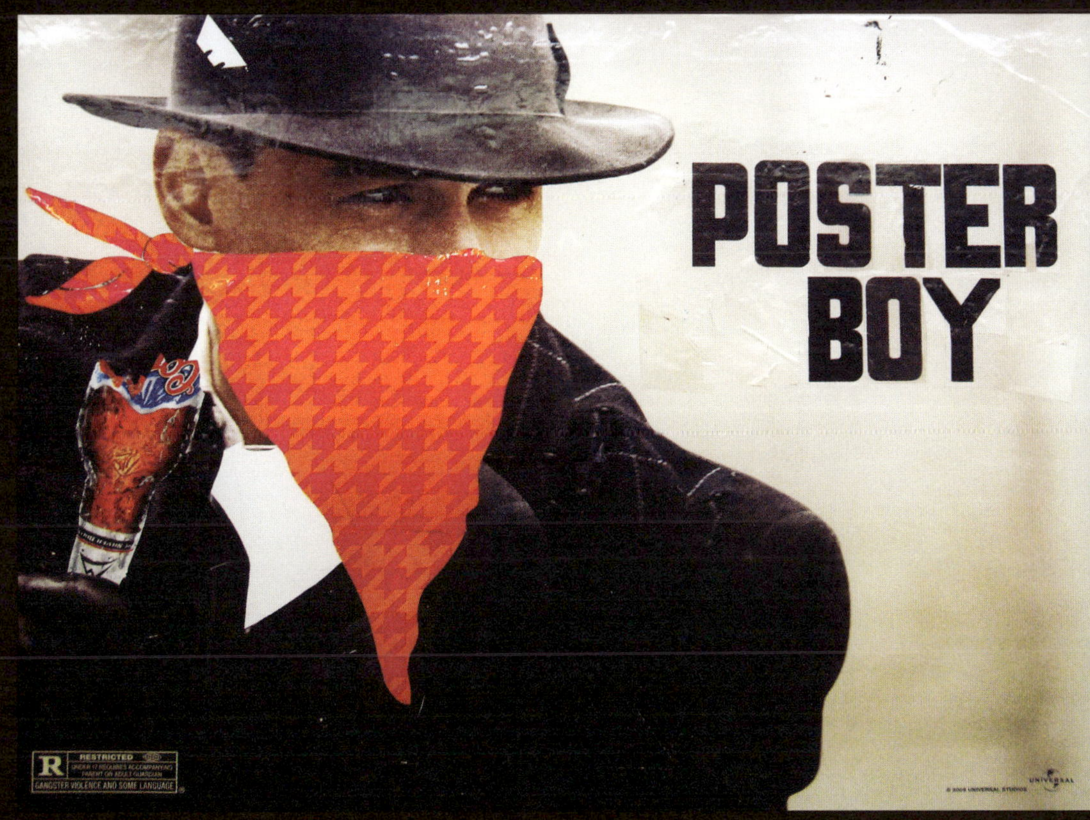

SELF-PORTRAIT

Johnny Depp hasn't gotten back to us about starring in the new Poster Boy movie.

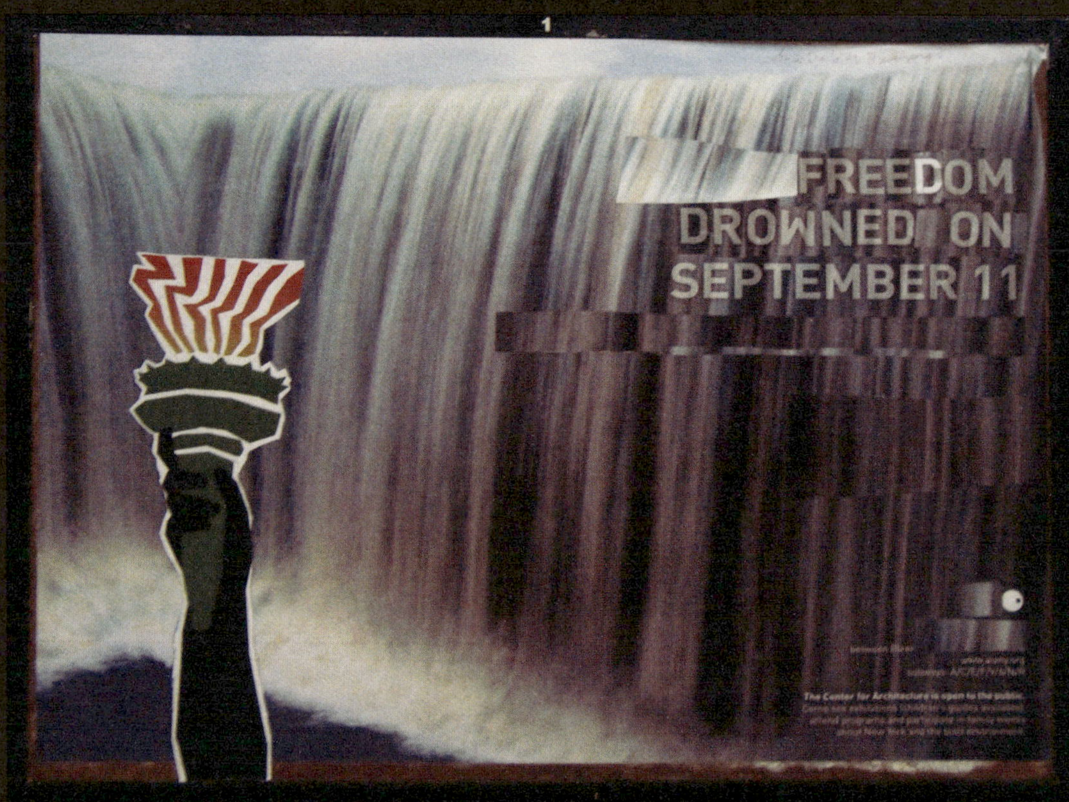
1
FREEDOM
DROWNED ON
SEPTEMBER 11

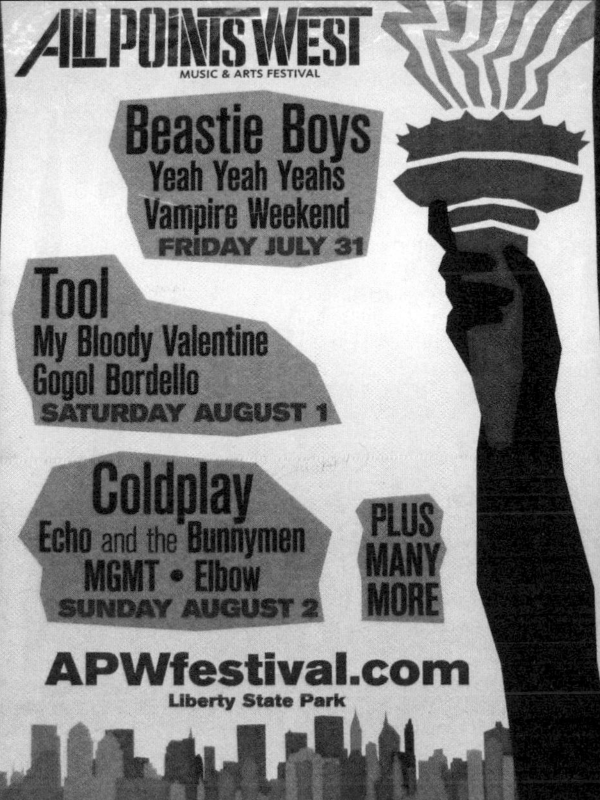

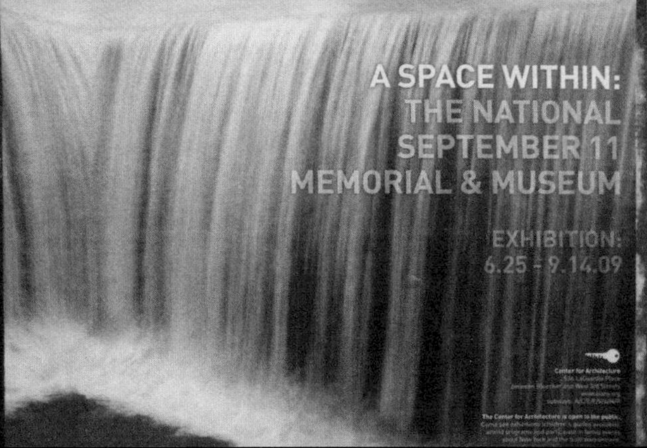

WHAT WENT DOWN?

There're still unanswered and unasked questions about the events surrounding the attacks on September 11th. Dwindling civil liberties and the terrorist witch hunt are all that have been certain since 9/11.

WHO'S PUNISHED

Like a "be back in five" sign, this poster serves as a gentle reminder of what New York's finest are capable of. Just ask the families of Amadou Diallo and Sean Bell.

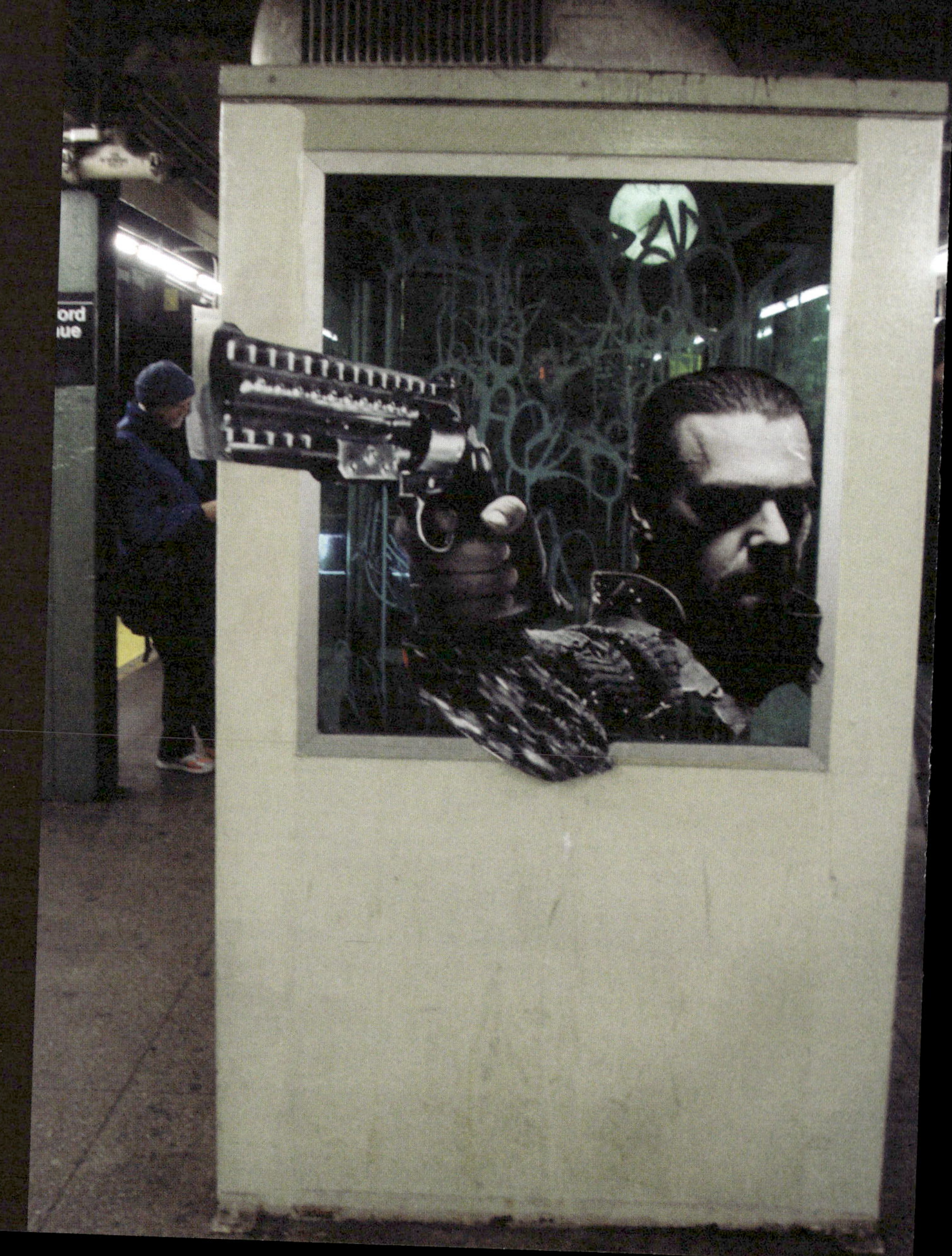

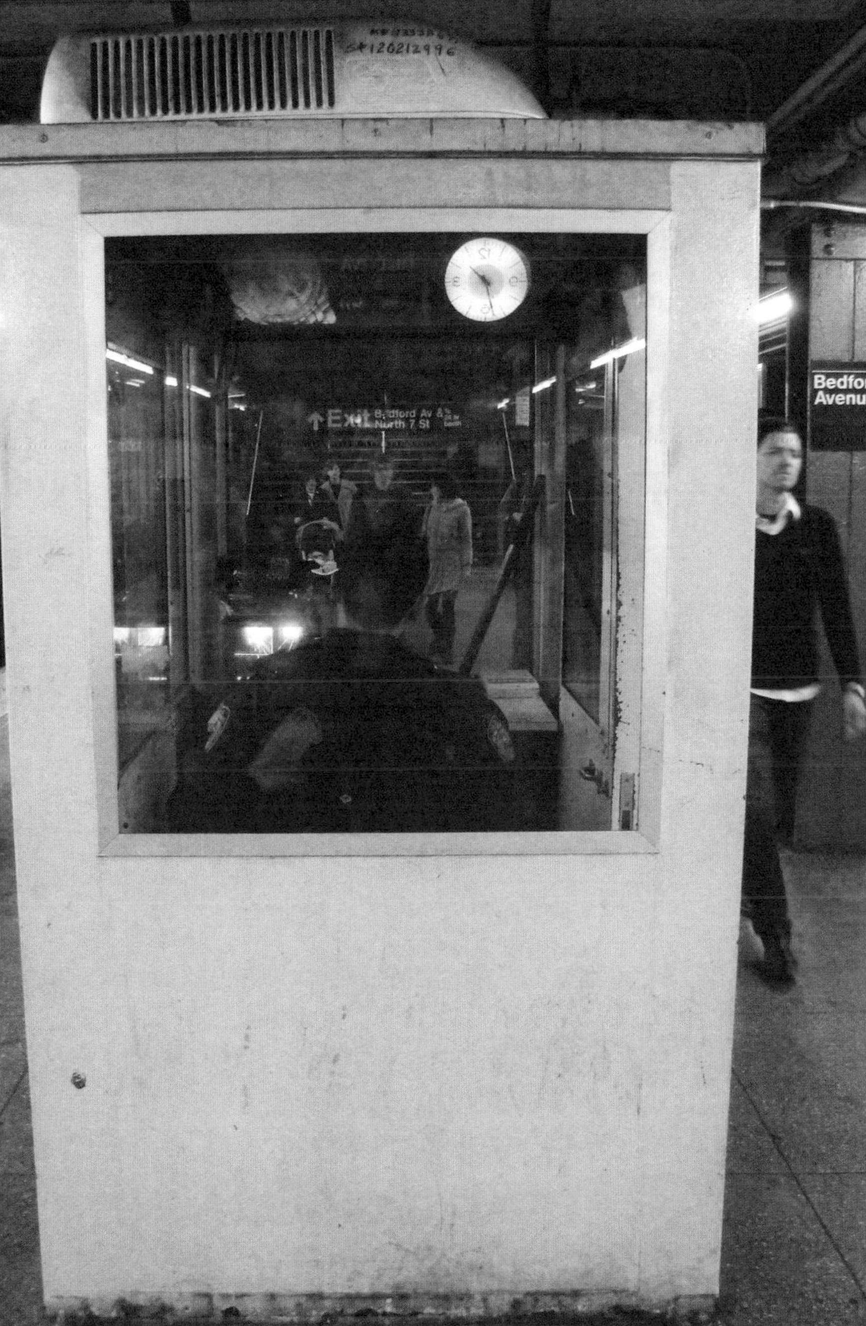

Exit
North 7 St
Bedford
Avenue

YELLOW WIZ ROAD

I mean come on! This one was too easy.

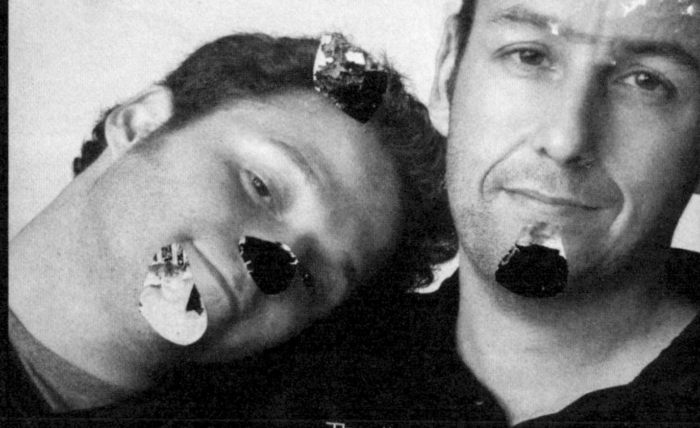

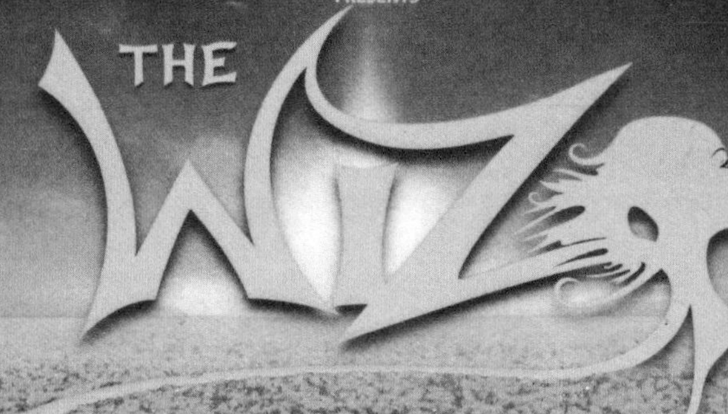

FREE!

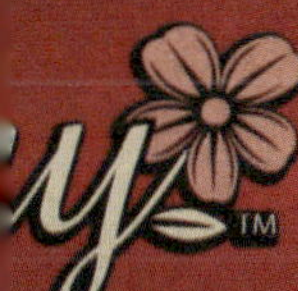

NEW YORK CITY CENTER 2009 *ENCORES!* SUMMER STARS Jack Viertel, Artistic Director

PRESENTS

THE WIZ

ASHANTI ORLANDO JONES

IN

THE WIZ

BOOK BY
WILLIAM F. BROWN

MUSIC & LYRICS BY
CHARLIE SMALLS

BASED ON THE STORY
"THE WONDERFUL WIZARD OF OZ" BY **L. Frank Baum**

STARRING
JOSHUA HENRY JAMES MONROE IGLEHART CHRISTIAN WHITE
TICHINA ARNOLD DAWNN LEWIS
AND
LaCHANZE

CHOREOGRAPHY BY
ANDY BLANKENBUEHLER

MUSIC DIRECTOR
ALEX LACAMOIRE

DIRECTED BY
THOMAS KAIL

JUNE 12 – JULY 5

Summer STARS ENCORES!

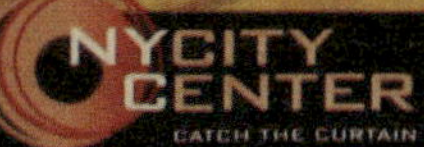

CITYTIX® 212.581.1212
NYCITYCENTER.ORG
WEST 55TH STREET (BTWN 6TH & 7TH)

Roz and Jerry Meyer
Ruthe and Tony Ponturo
Stephanie and Fred Shuman Fund for *Encores!*

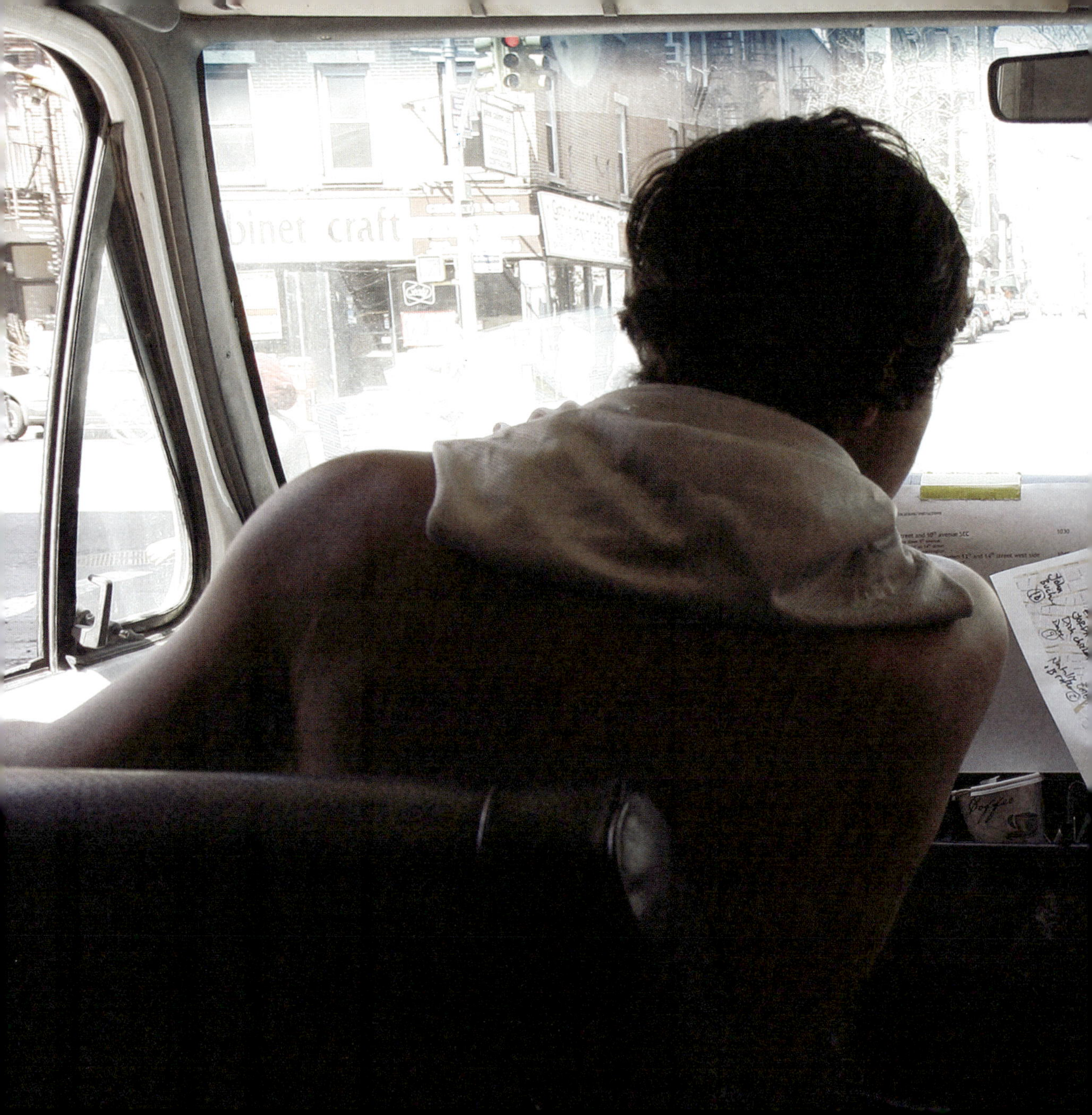
binet craft

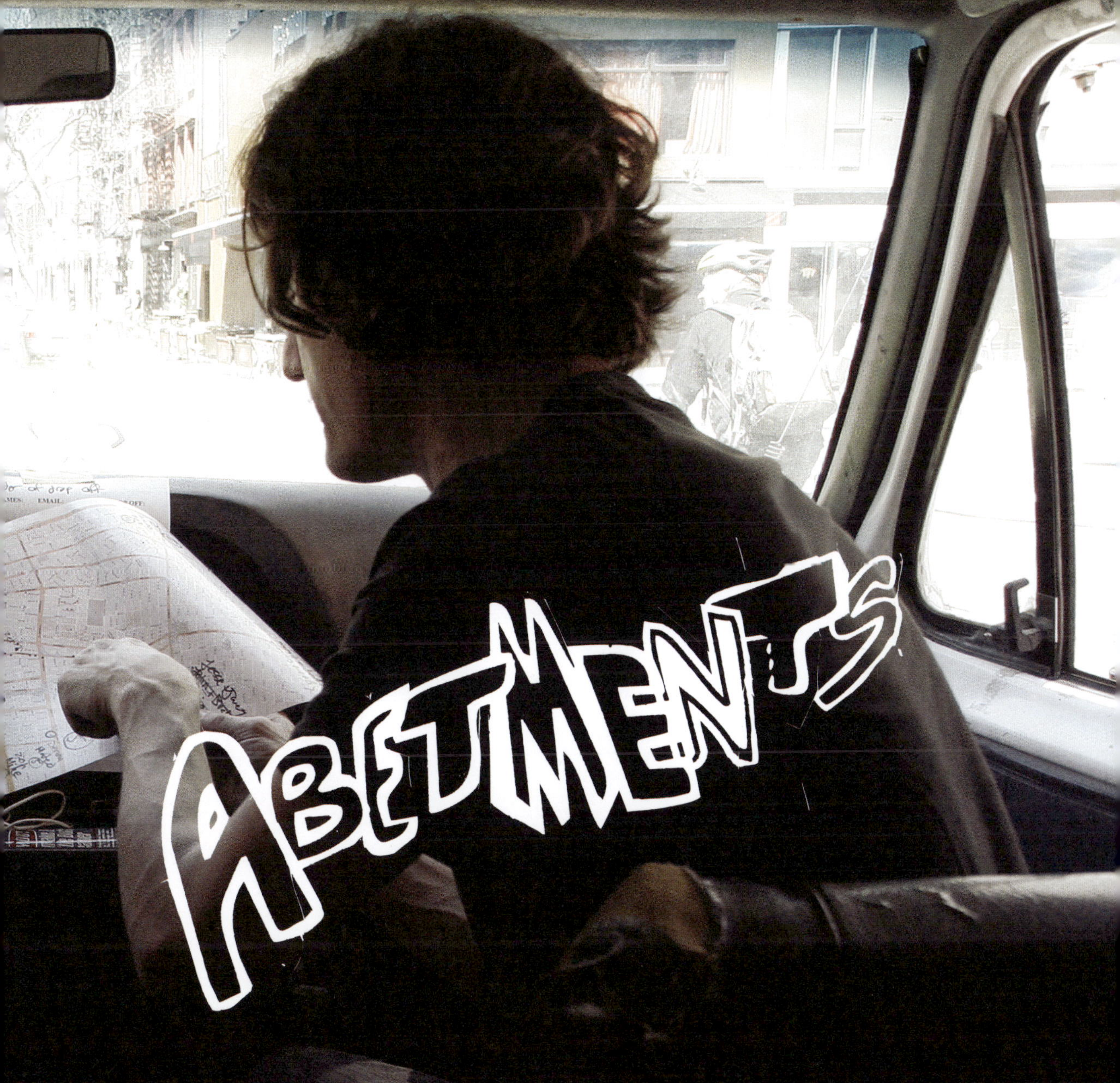
ABETMENTS

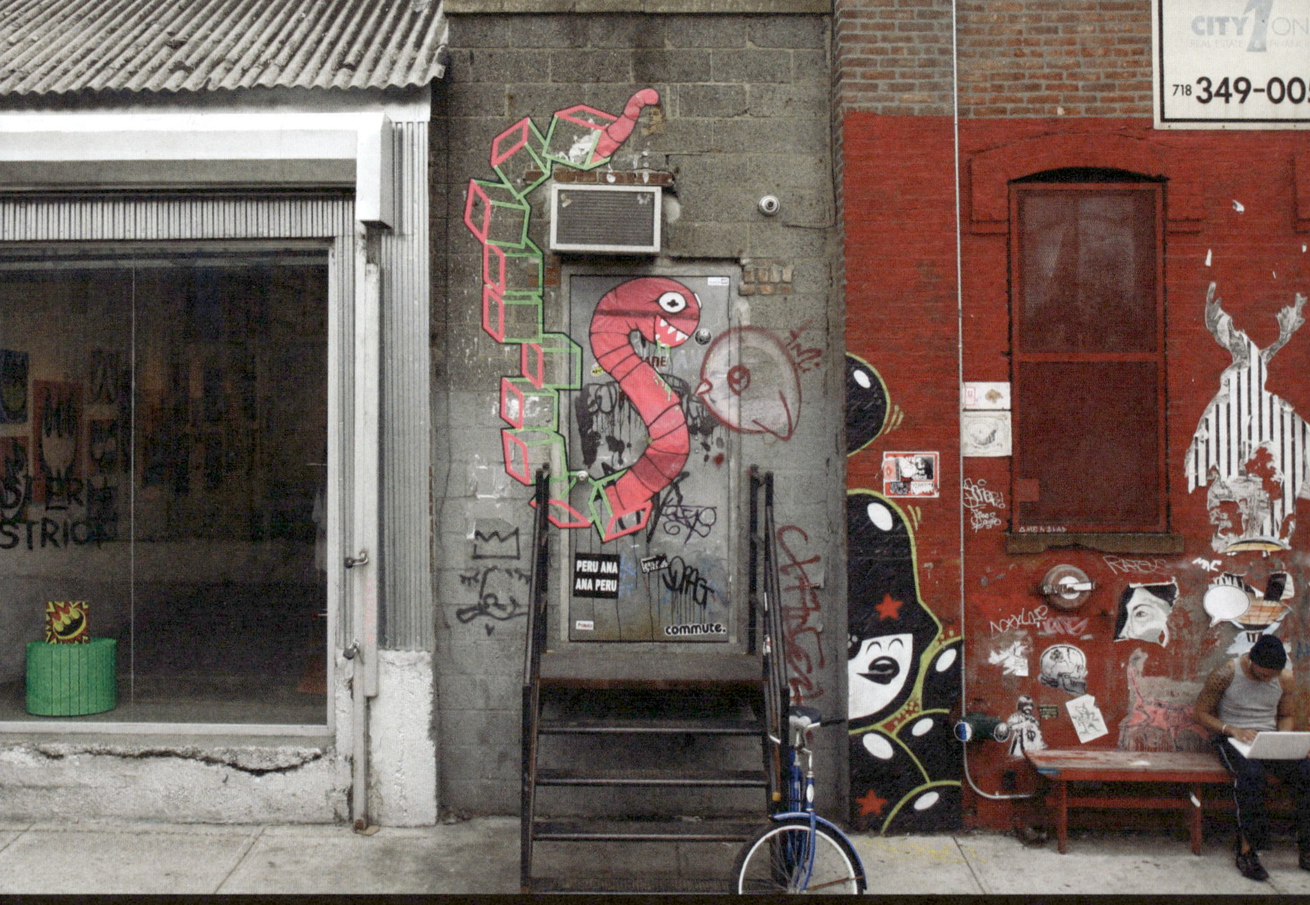

BURLY WORM GETS THE BIRD

During the solo show at Eastern District a little birdie visited the gallery's door. When the show came down the vinyl was used to create this response with Aakash Nihalani.

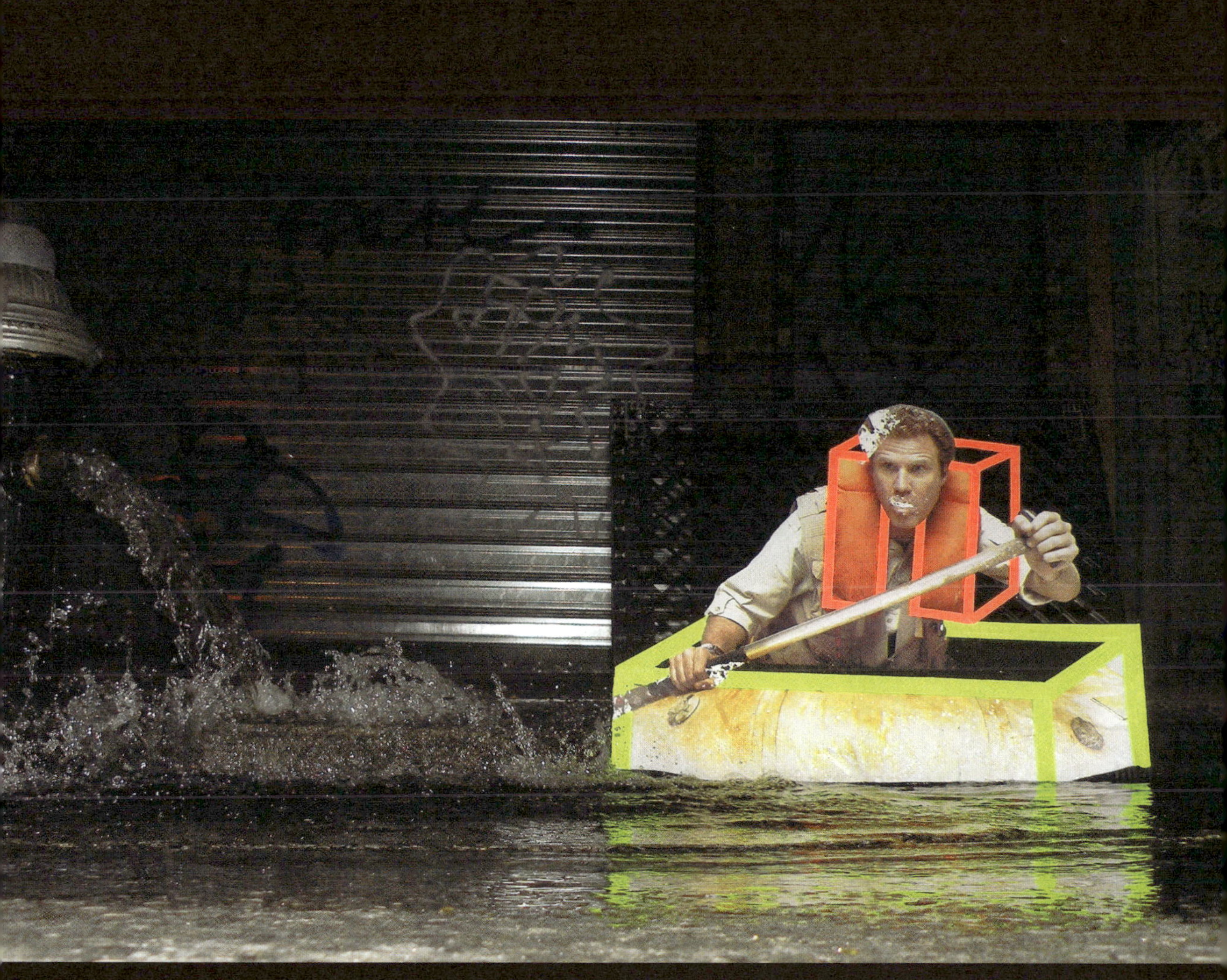

Photo courtesy of Aakash.

NIGHT WATER RAFTING

Opening a hydrant on a hot summer night is a result of boredom—so was this collaboration with Aakash Nihalani.

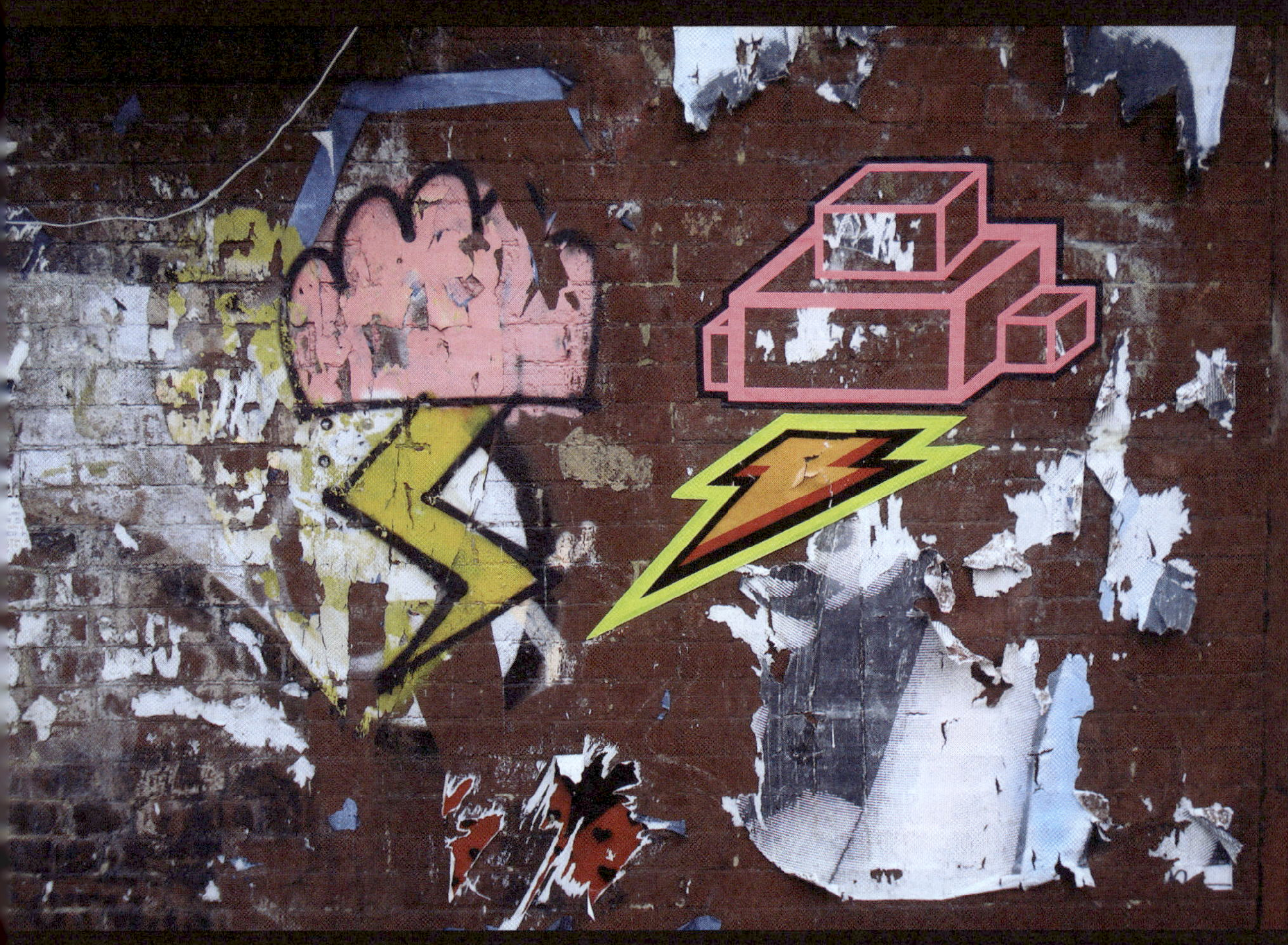

PINK CLOUD TRIBUTE

These electrolytes satisfy the eyes' thirst. (Collaboration with Aakash Nihalani.)

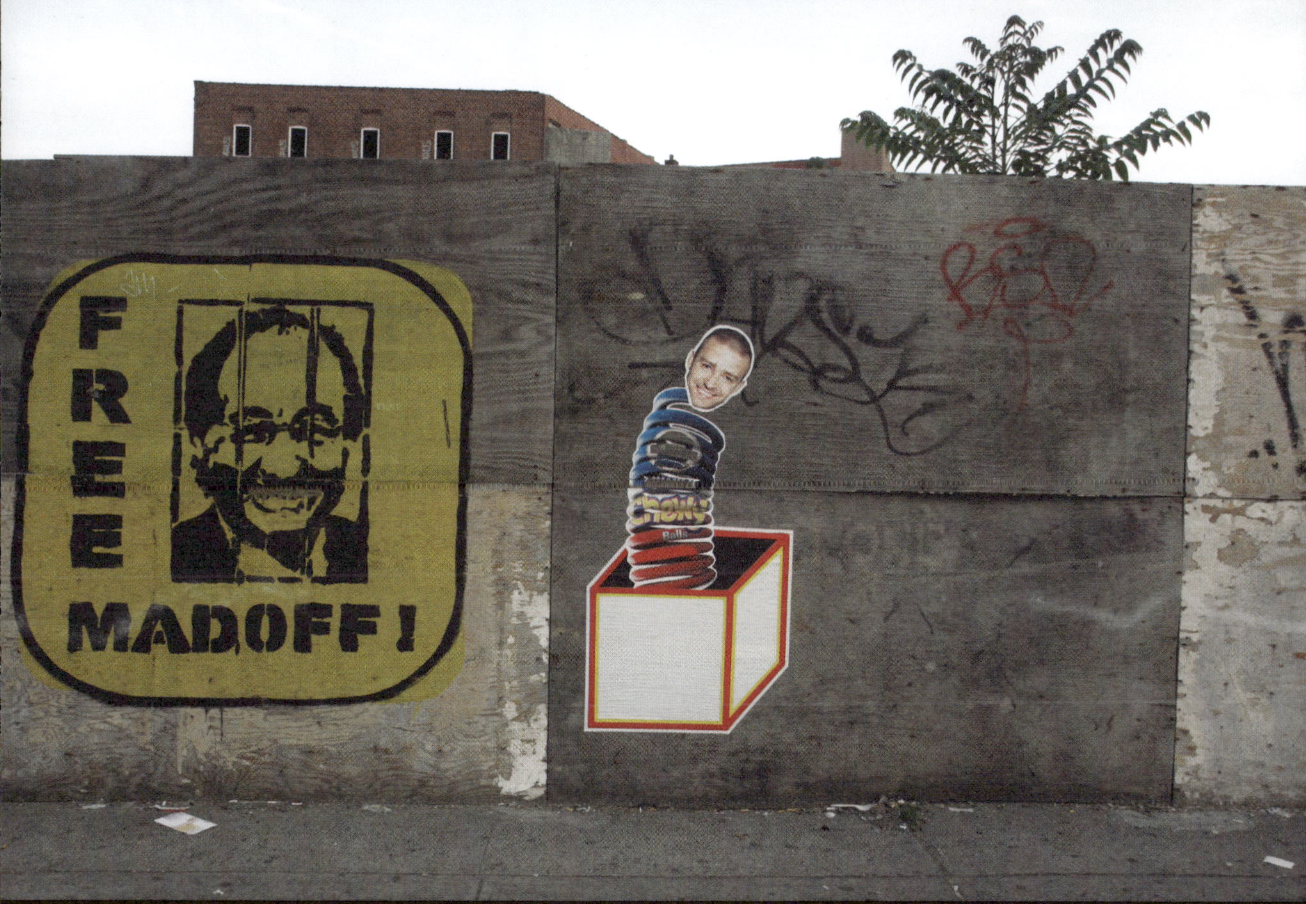

DICK IN A BOX

This parody of a parody renders the celebrity as the dick. (Collaboration with Aakash Nihalani.)

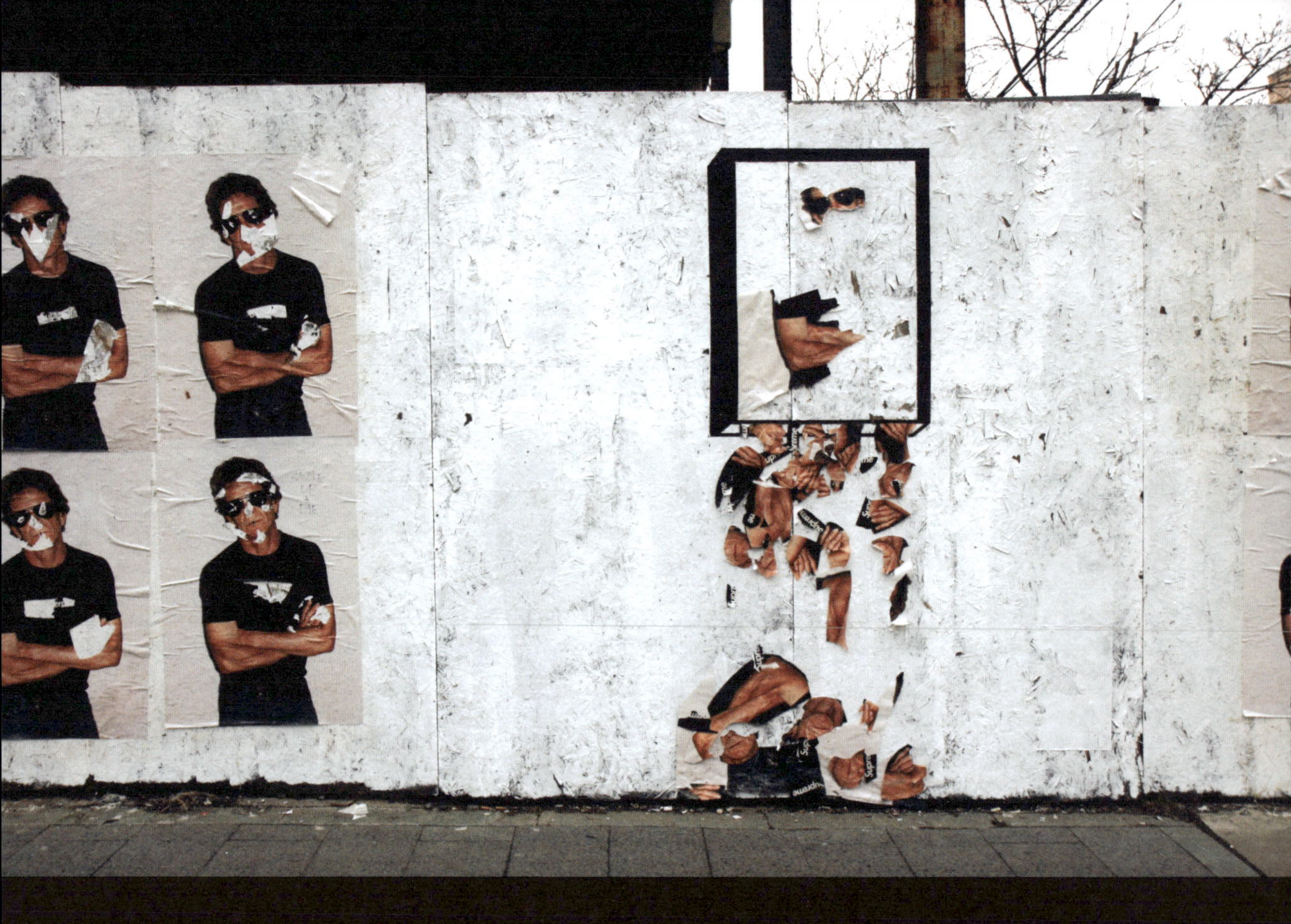

VINYL UNDERGROUND

Lou—you helped invent NYC cool, no doubt about it. But dude, get over yourself.

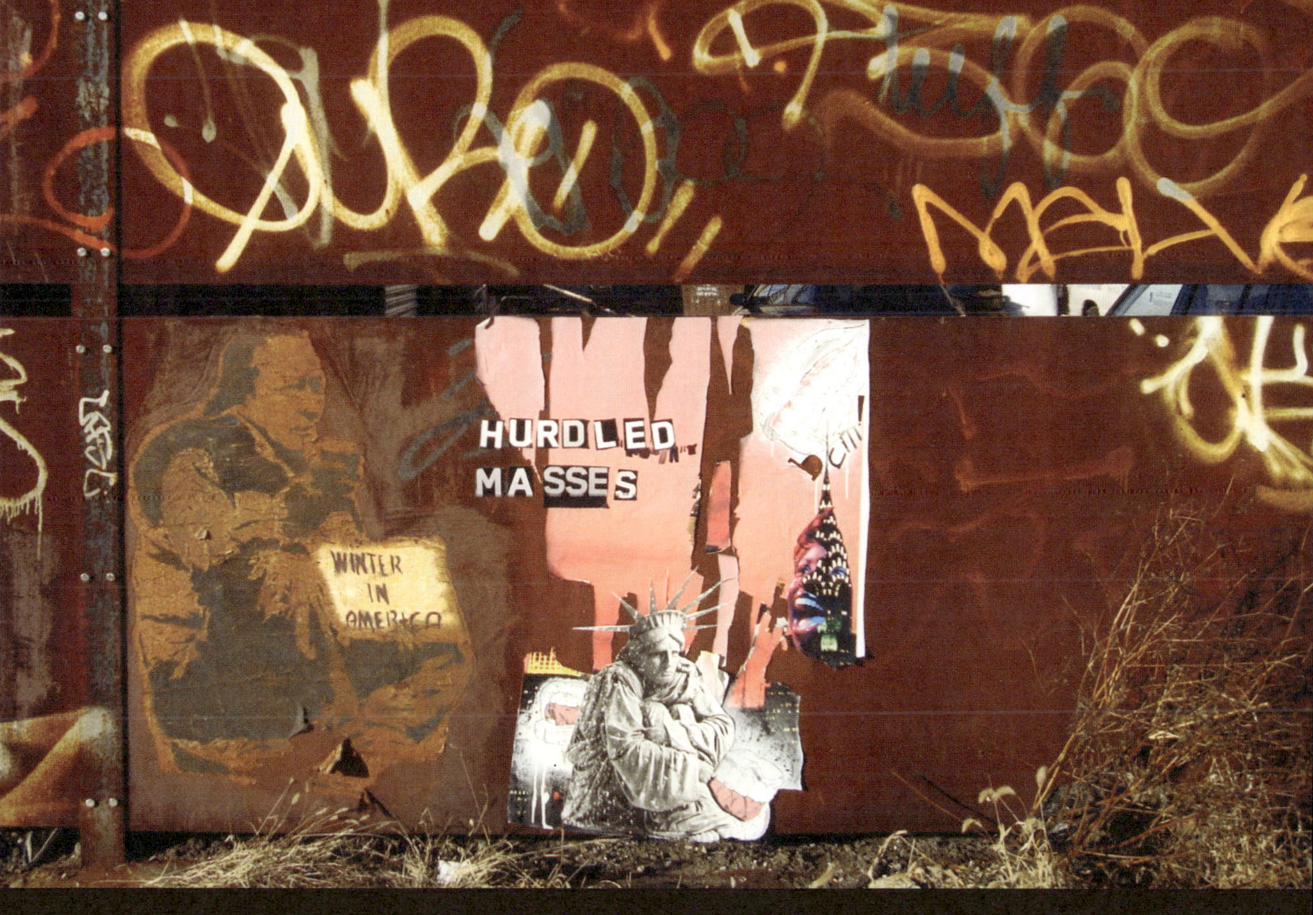

HURDLED MASSES

This collaboration with street artist NohJColey was created to accompany a beautifully faded Chris Stain paste-up.

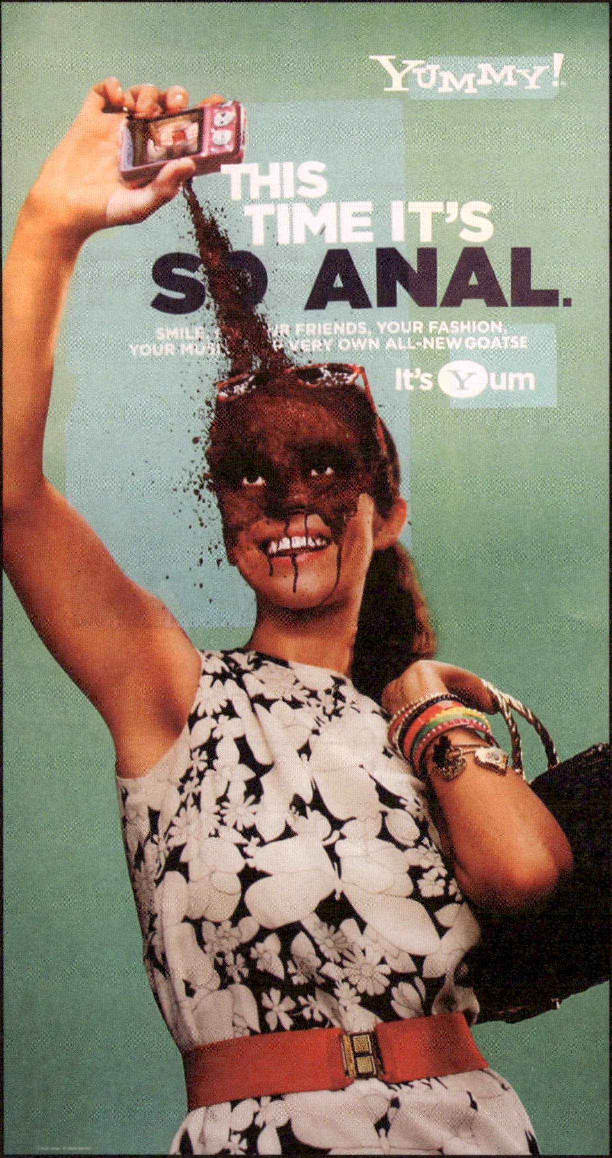

YUMMY!

THIS
TIME IT'S
SO ANAL.

SMILE. ...R FRIENDS, YOUR FASHION,
YOUR MUSI... VERY OWN ALL-NEW GOATSE

It's Yum

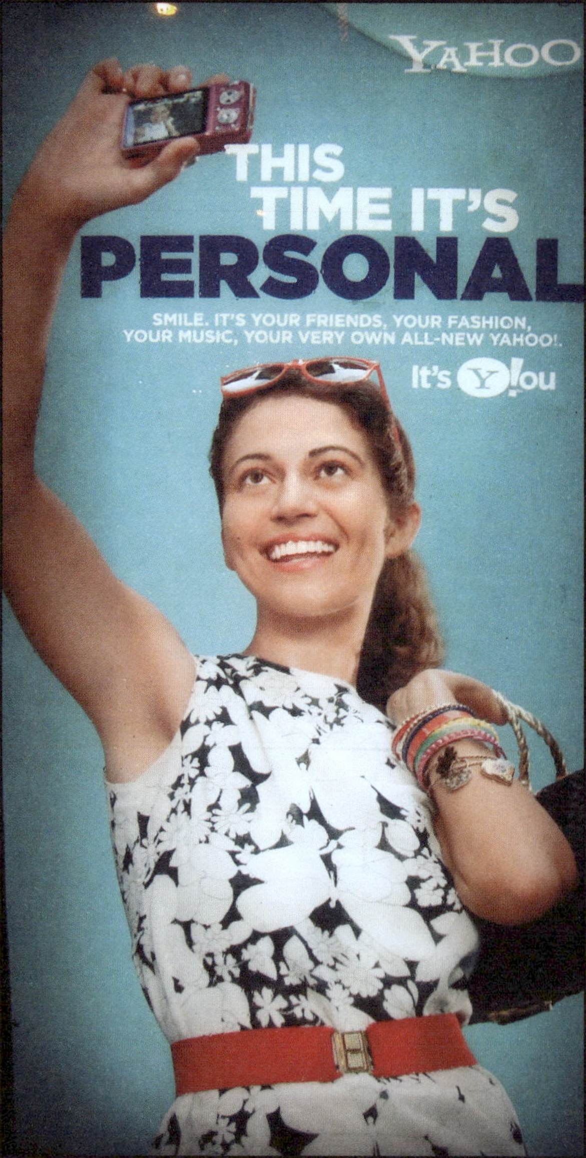

YAHOO

THIS
TIME IT'S
PERSONAL

SMILE. IT'S YOUR FRIENDS, YOUR FASHION,
YOUR MUSIC, YOUR VERY OWN ALL-NEW YAHOO!.

It's Y!ou

GOATSE/SHITFLOP

Poster Boy and the UK's Decapitator join forces to form *Decrapitator!*

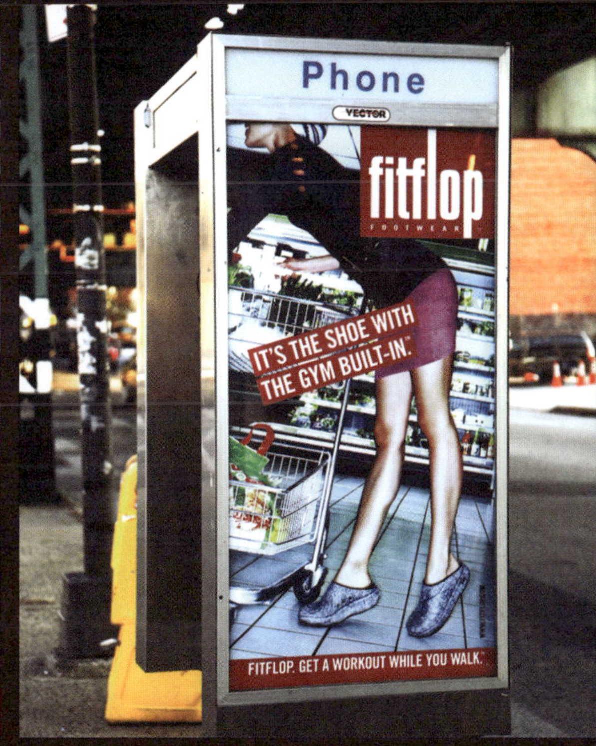

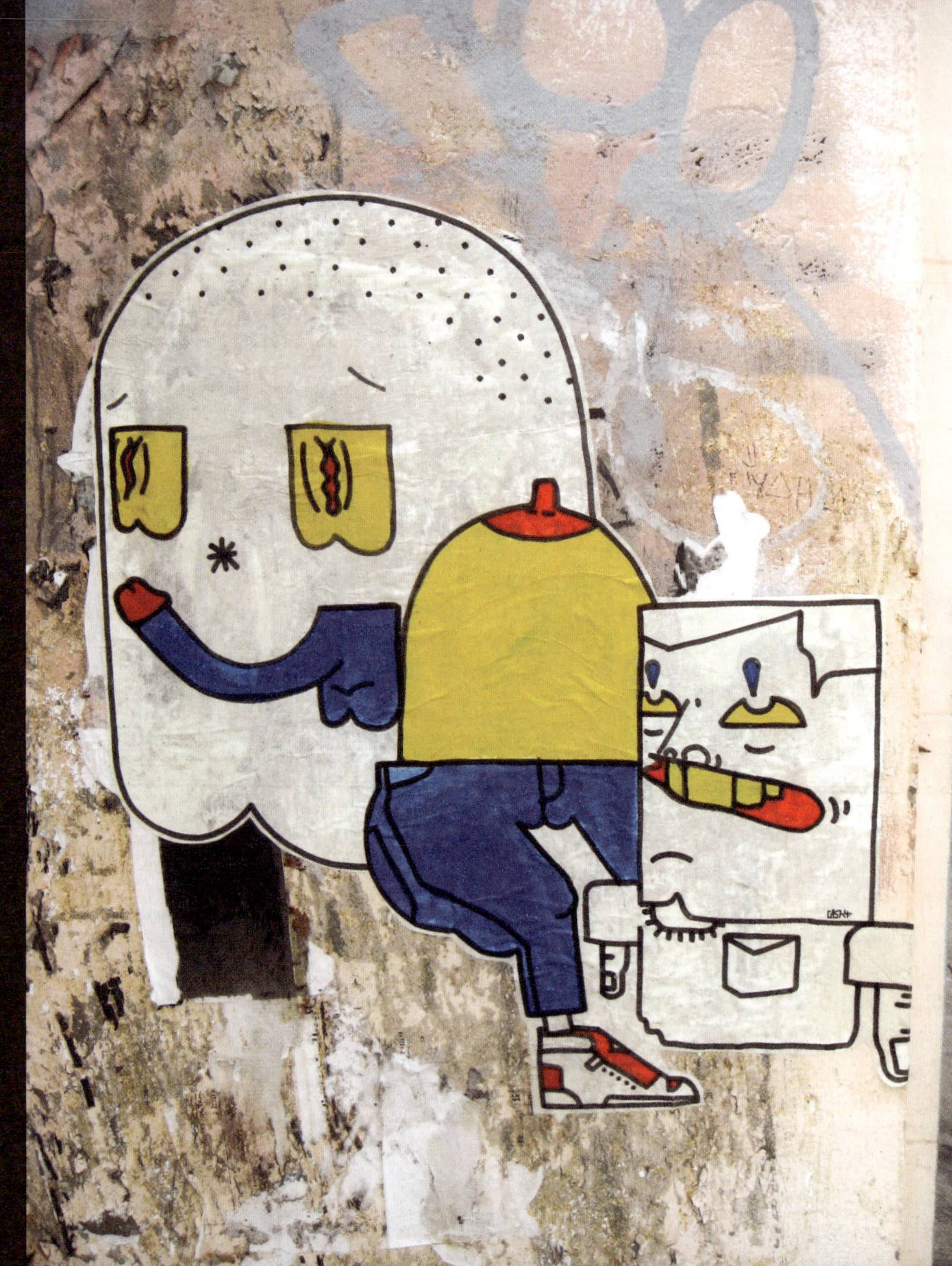

Photo courtesy of CASH 4.

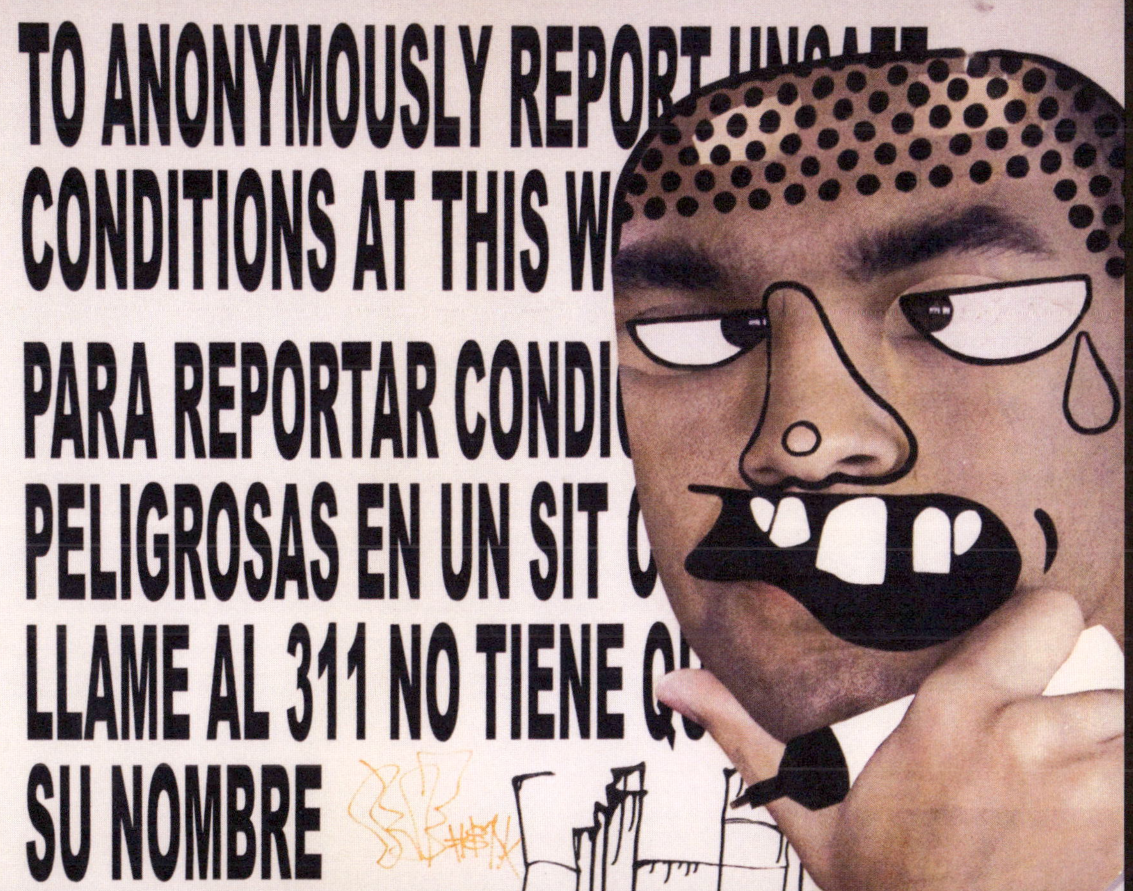

WHAT'S CA$H 4?

A tribute to graffiti artist CA$H 4, in the fashion of his trademark head/portrait style. Ironically, it's over a CA$H 4 tag.

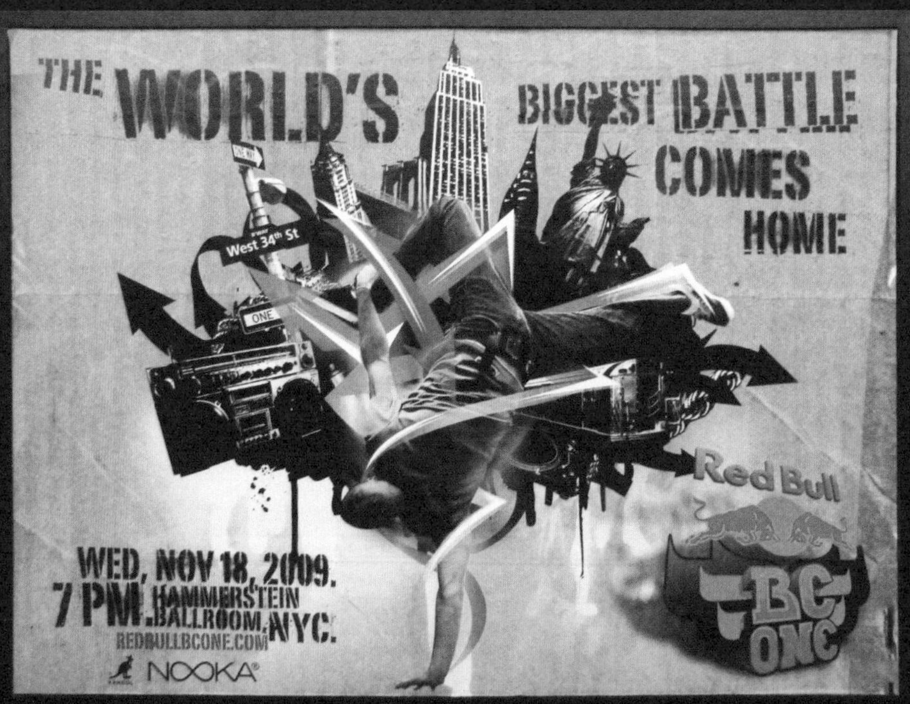

FUCK HIP-POP

The graffiti legend Mare 139's commissioned "Hip-Hop" poster was repurposed as embellishment for this already stunning Dude Company stencil that honors the MC Black Thought.

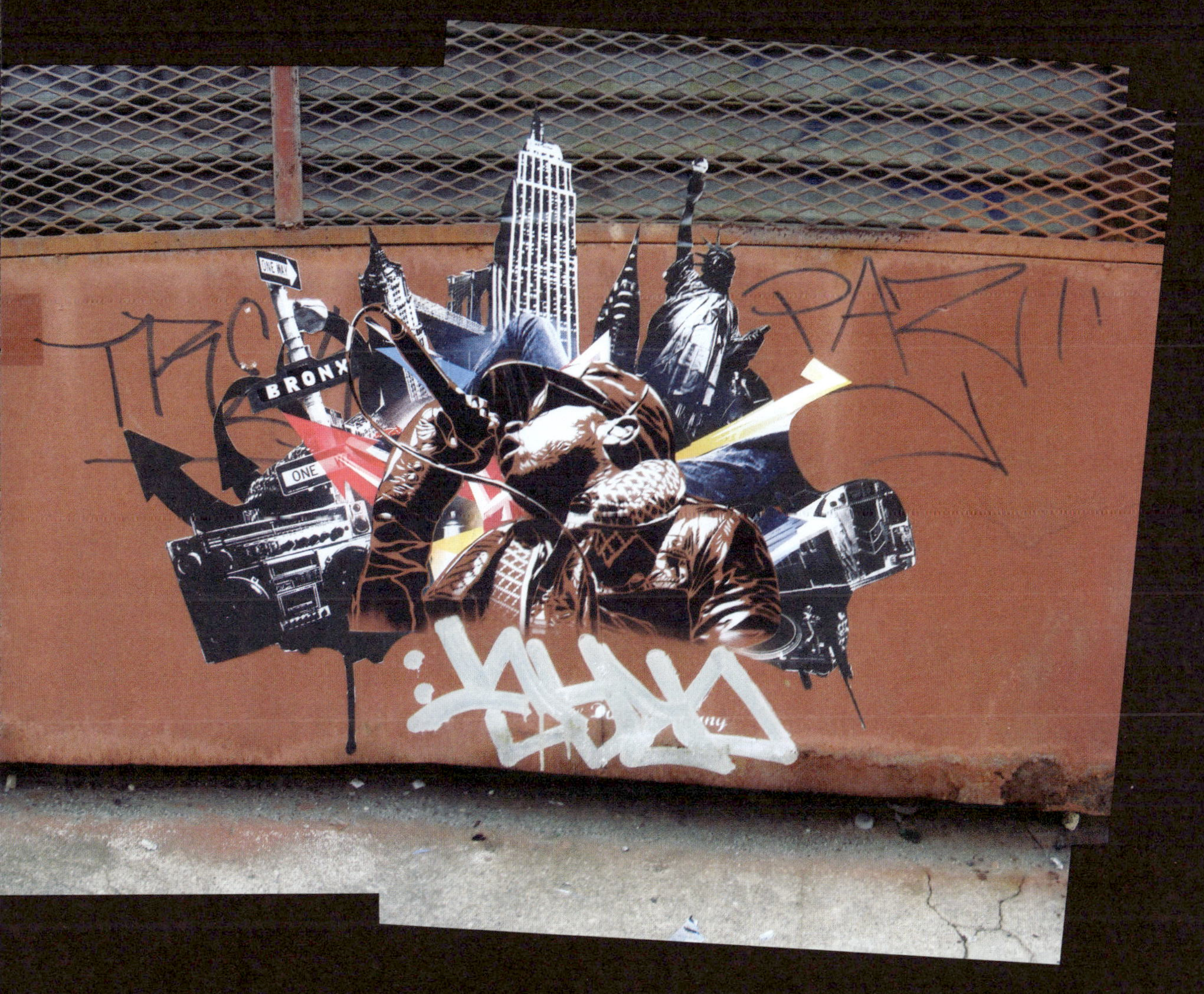
ONE WAY
BRONX
ONE

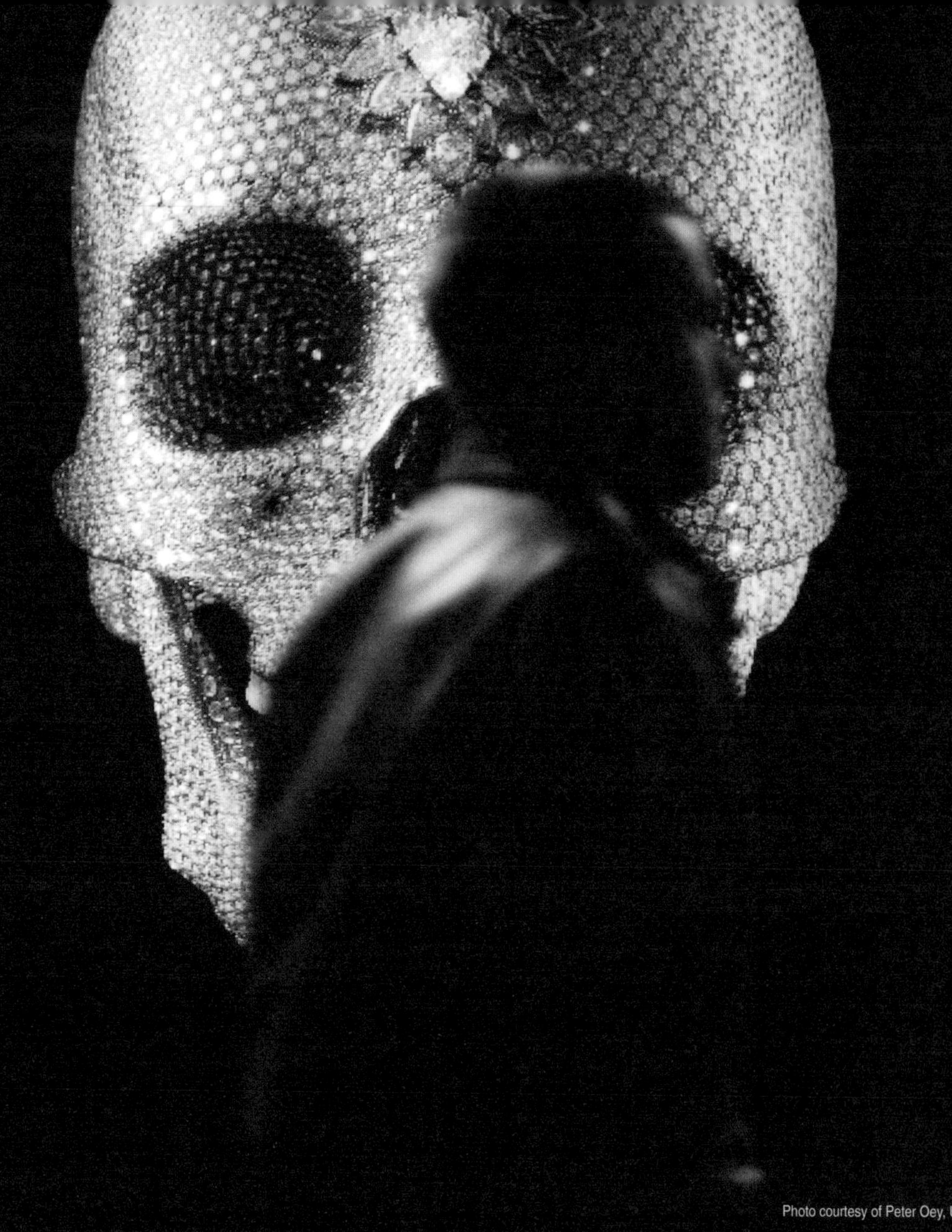

Photo courtesy of Peter Oey, Utrecht.

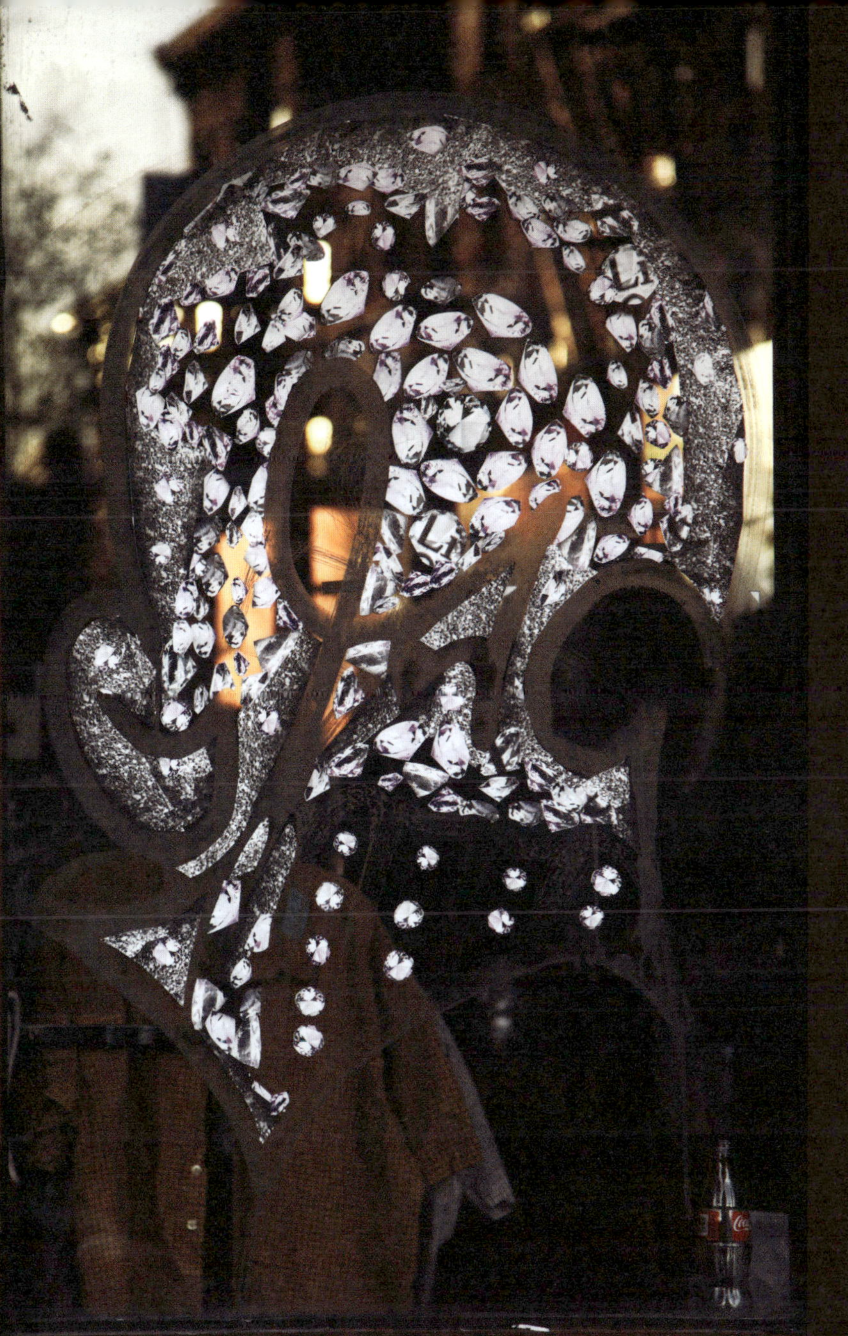

FOR THE LOVE OF THE SPECTACLE

A tribute to one of Brooklyn's finest, Katsu. The diamonds were mined from about 30 posters. The cops came before the skull could be fully blinged-out.

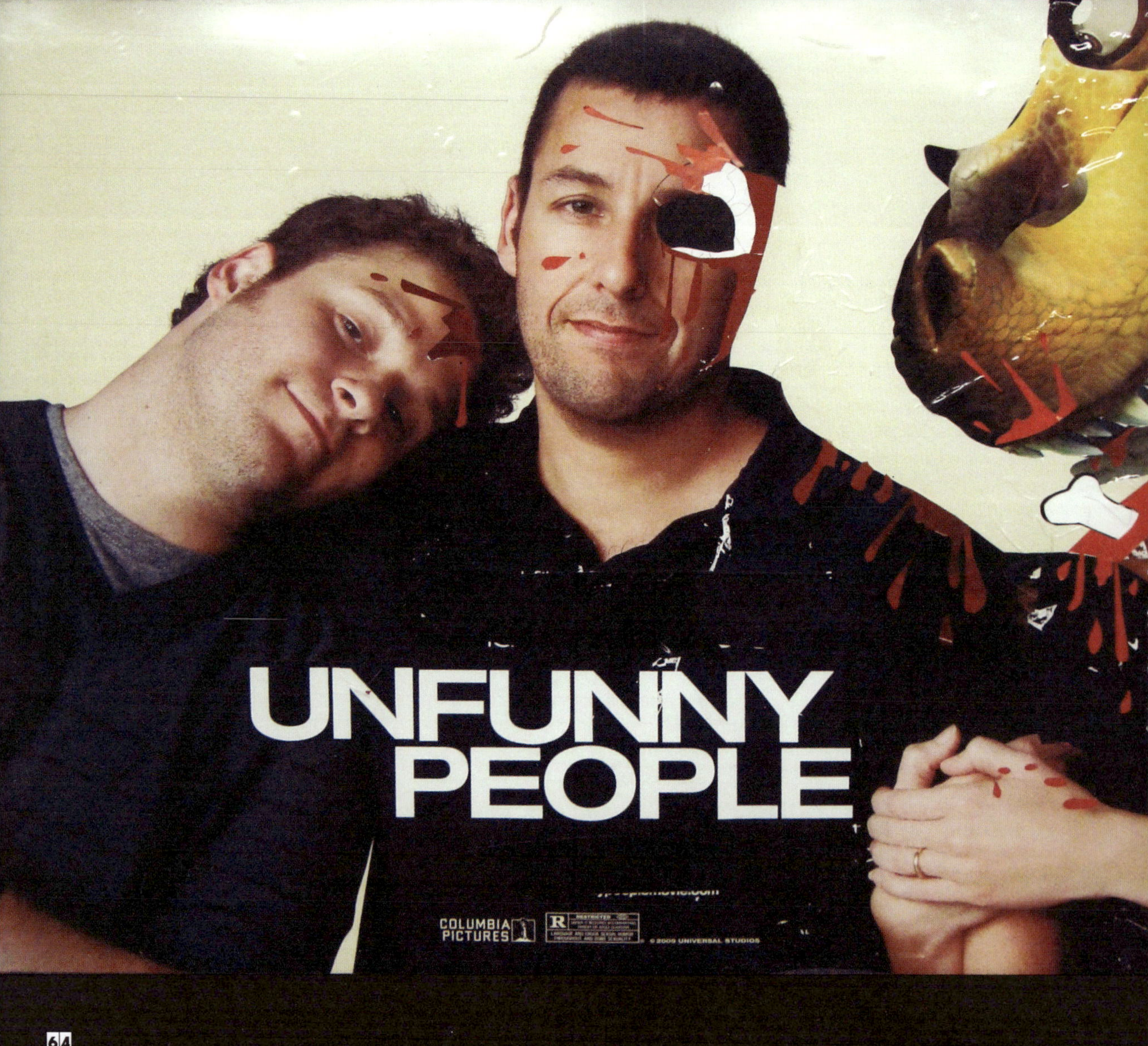
UNFUNNY
PEOPLE
COLUMBIA
PICTURES
R
RESTRICTED
© 2009 UNIVERSAL STUDIOS

DECAPITATOR TRIBUTE

A tribute to the Zorro of the UK.

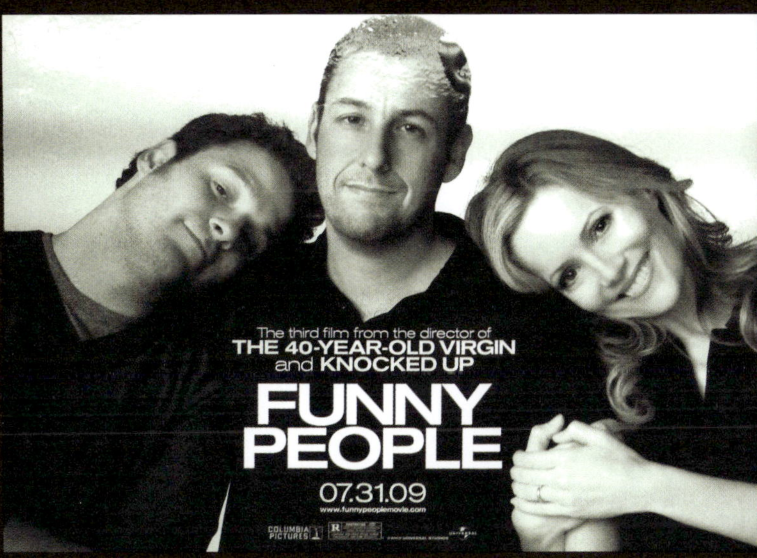

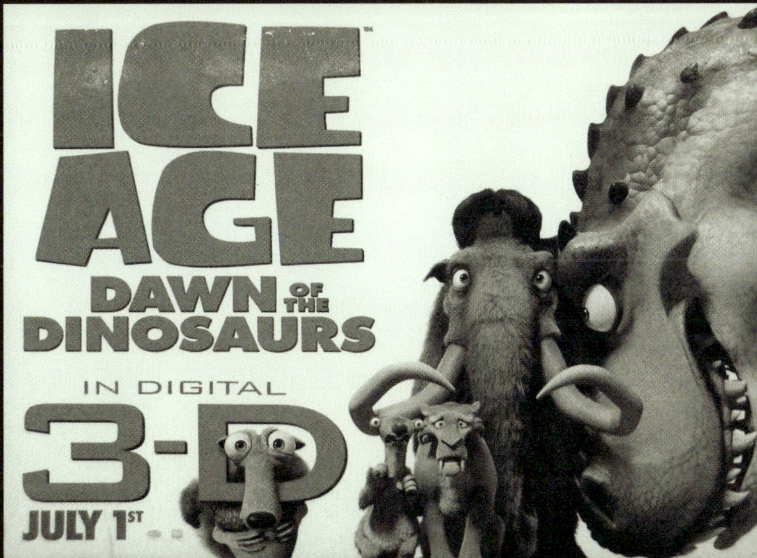

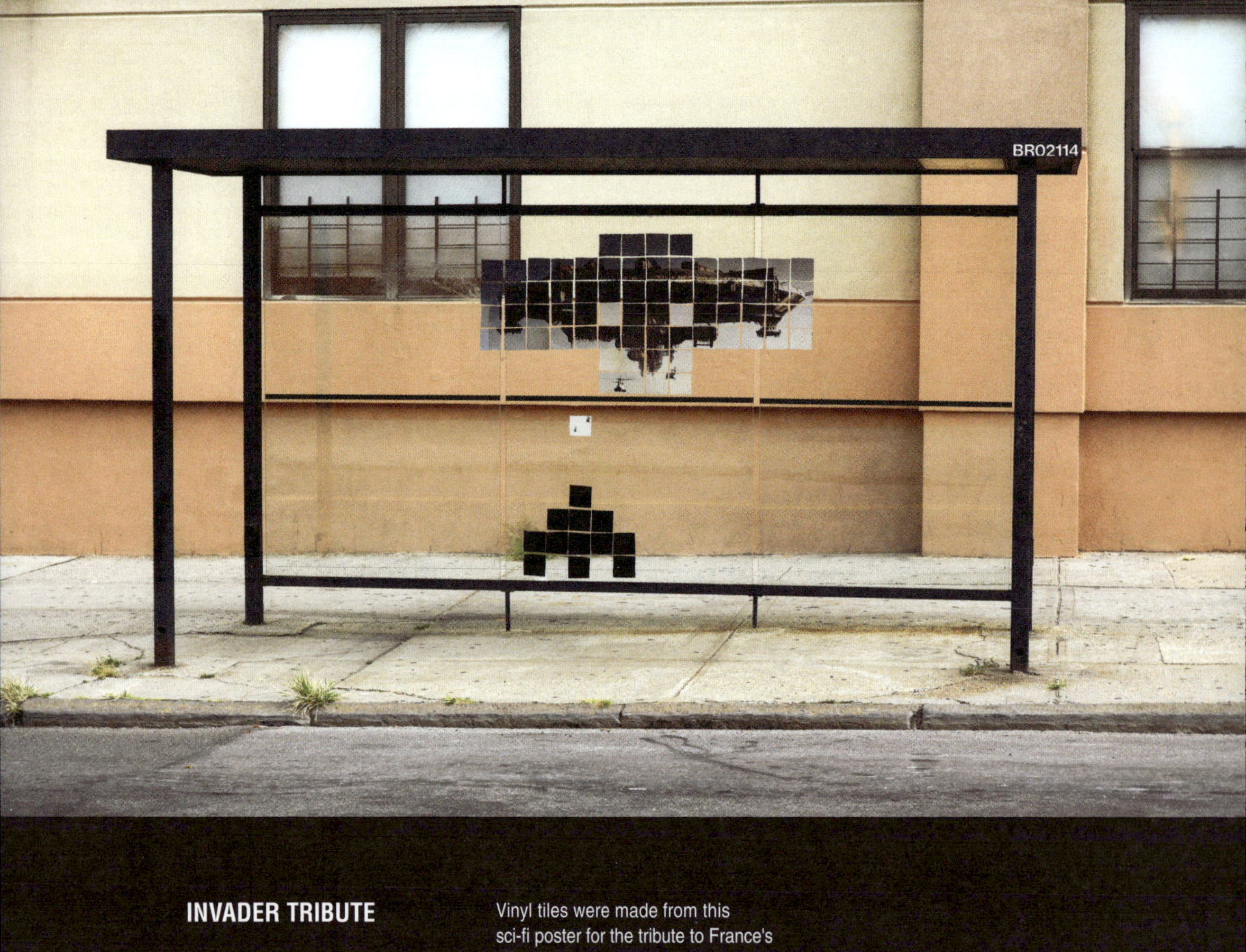

INVADER TRIBUTE

Vinyl tiles were made from this sci-fi poster for the tribute to France's premier tile street artist.

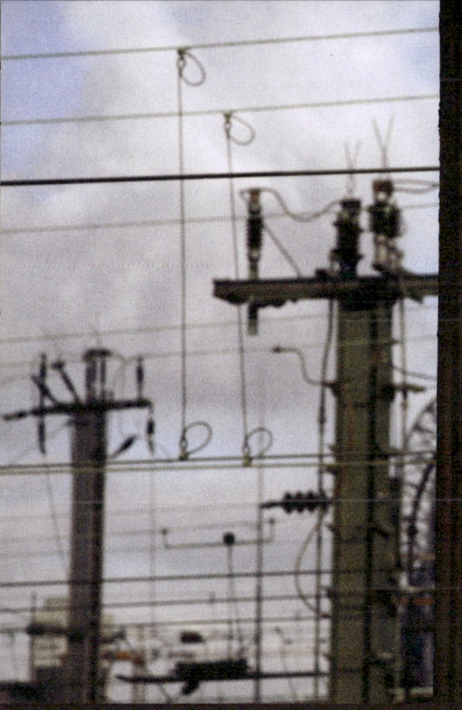

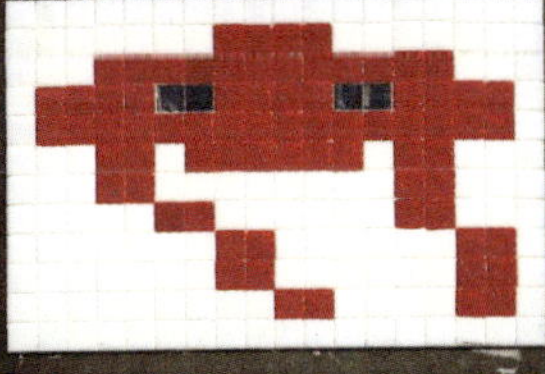

KLN_19 (Cologne, 2006); Photo courtesy of Invader.

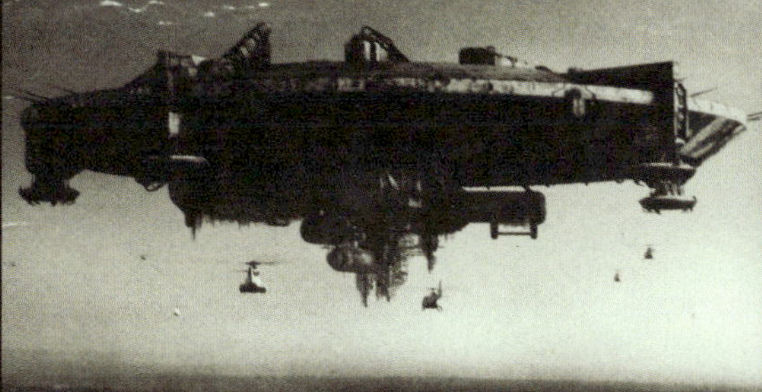

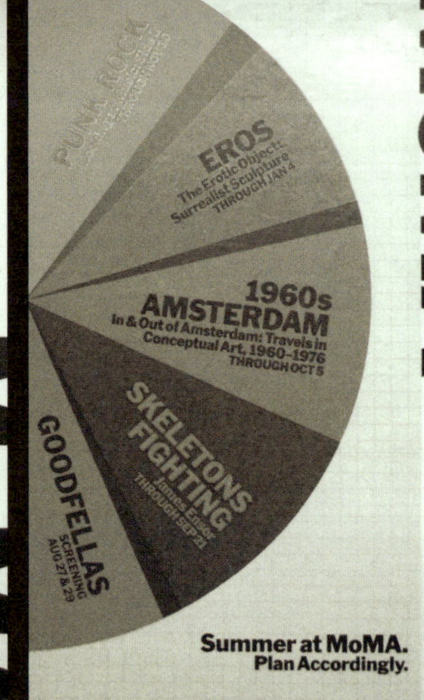

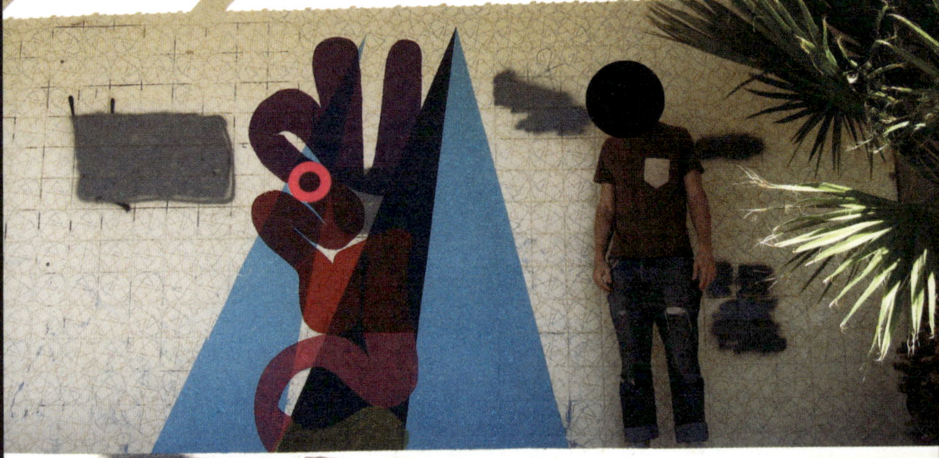

Photo courtesy of MOMO.

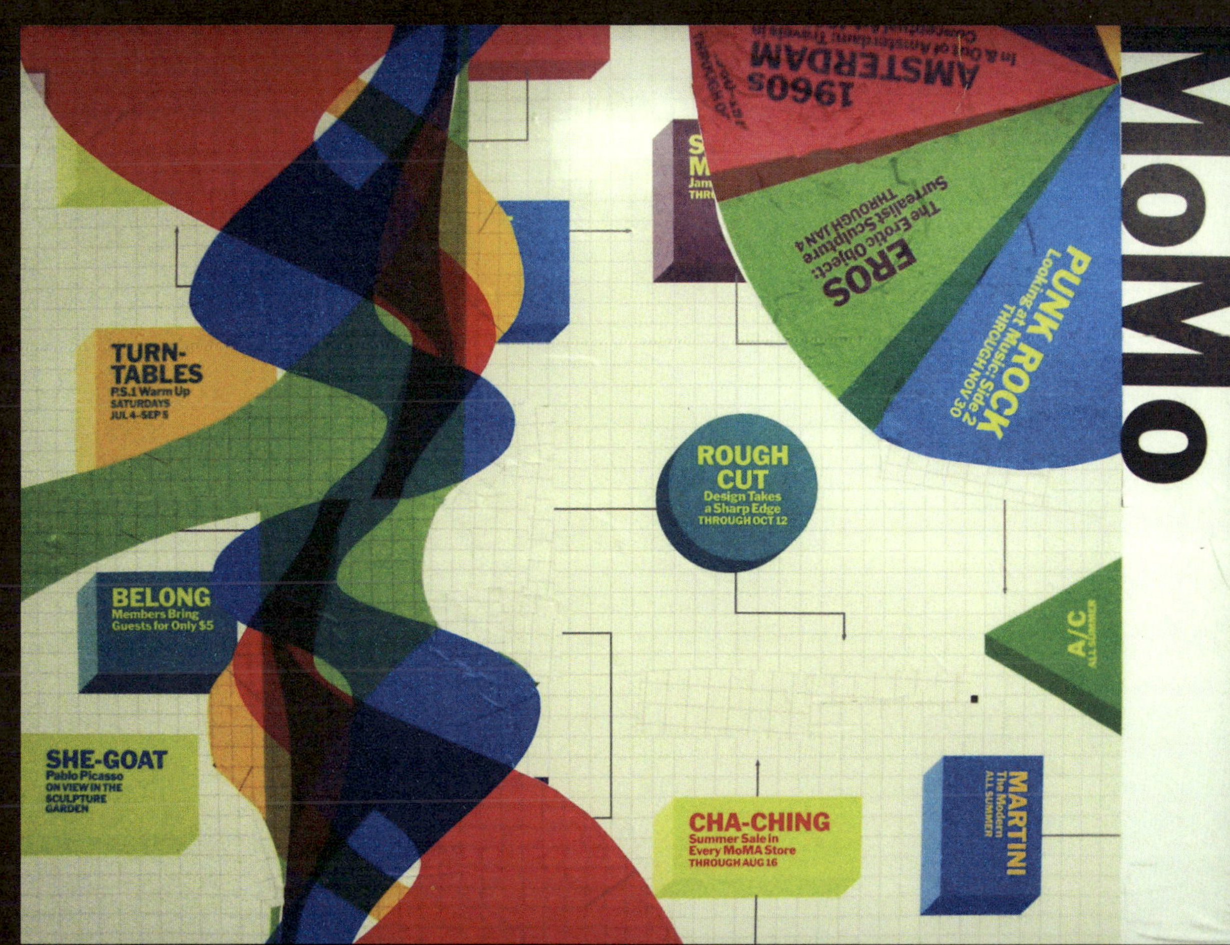

MOMO TRIBUTE

Momo's concept-heavy style prompted this tribute, and probably MoMA's campaign.

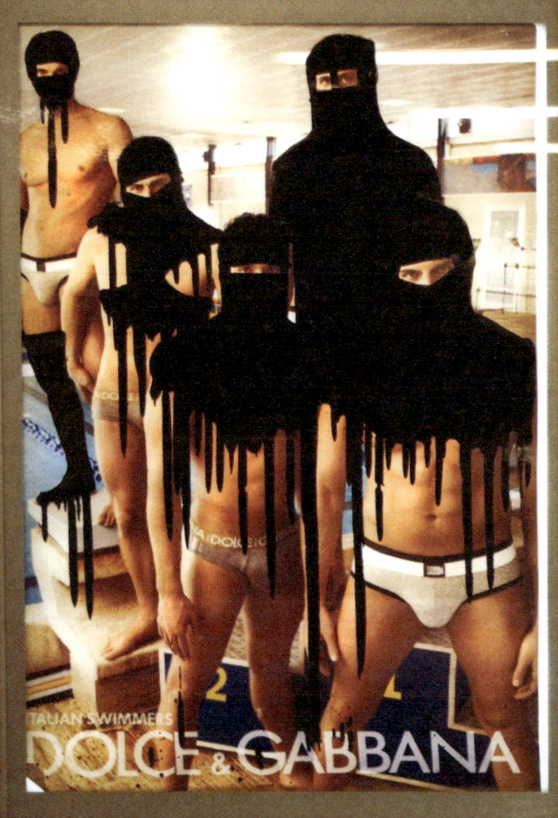

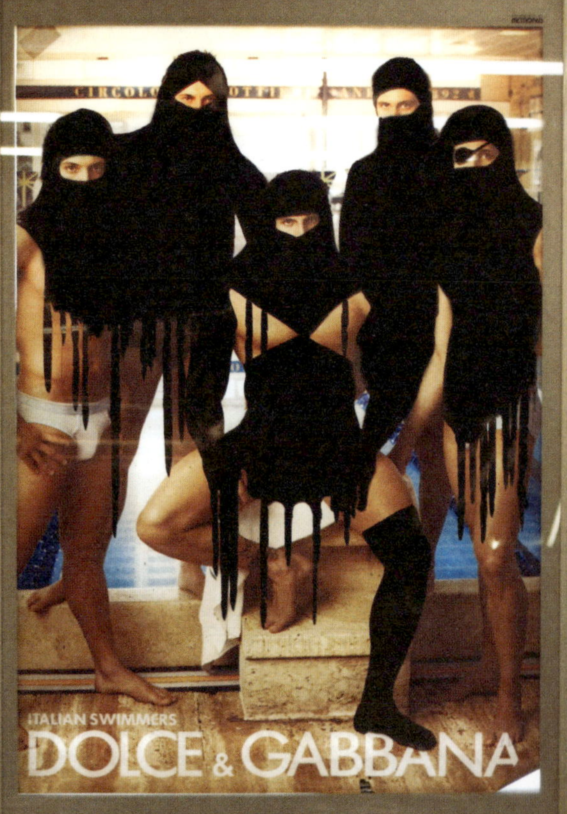

Photo courtesy of Princess Hijab.

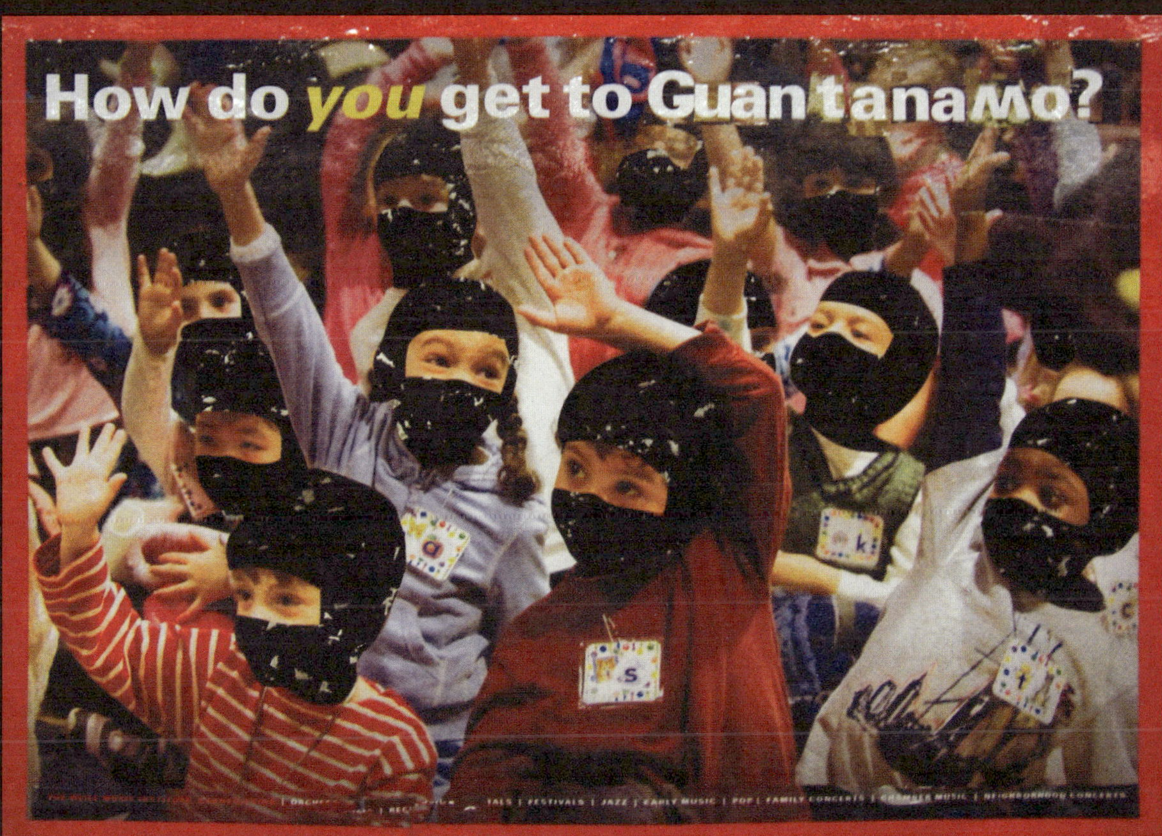

PRINCESS HIJAB TRIBUTE

Armed with the color black, Princess Hijab is able to turn any ad on its head with a few swift moves. The sentiments are reciprocated.

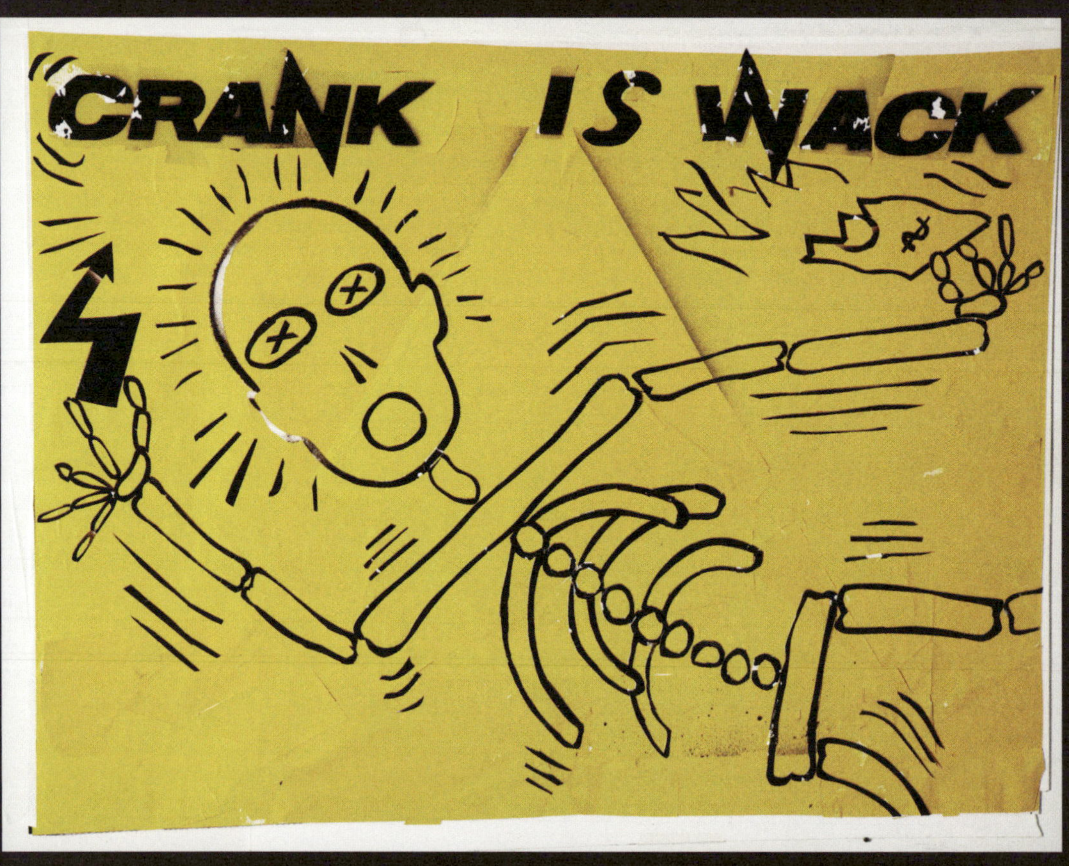

KEITH HARING TRIBUTE

The original subway artist is given his due while commenting on the crack of our day.

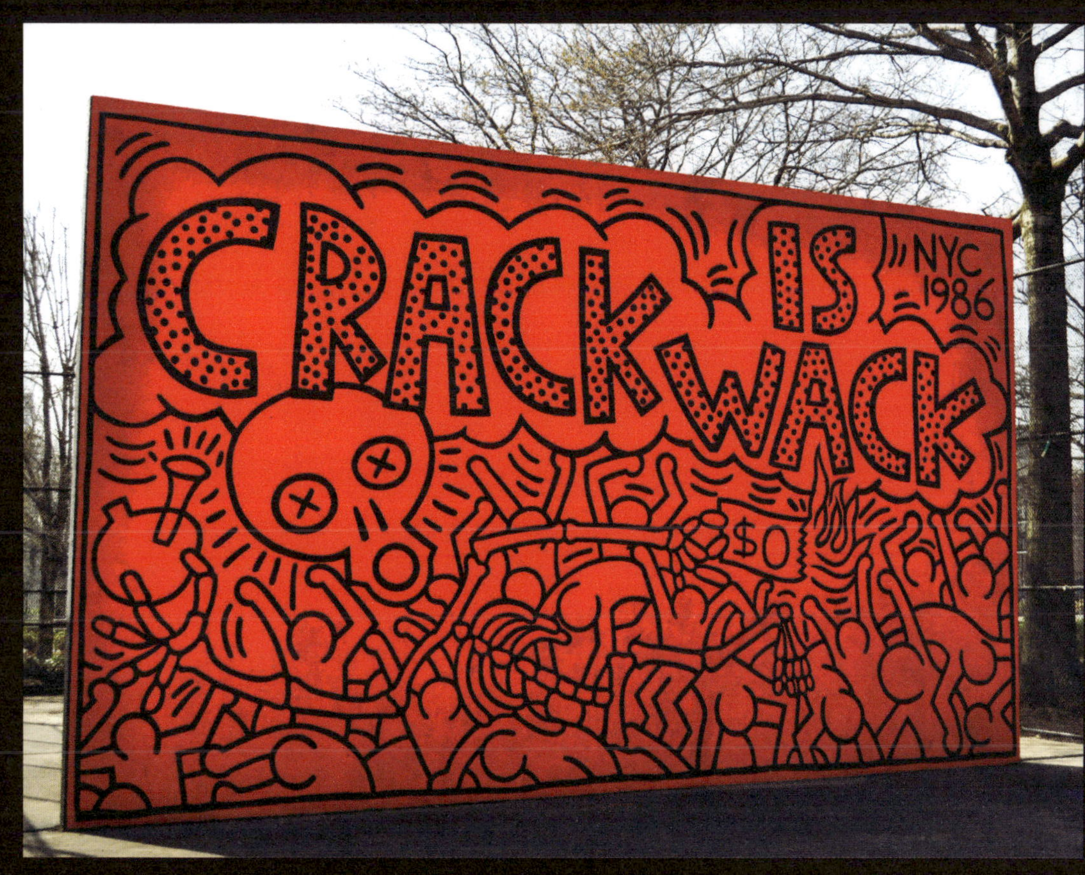

Photo courtesy of J. Cantrell Davis.

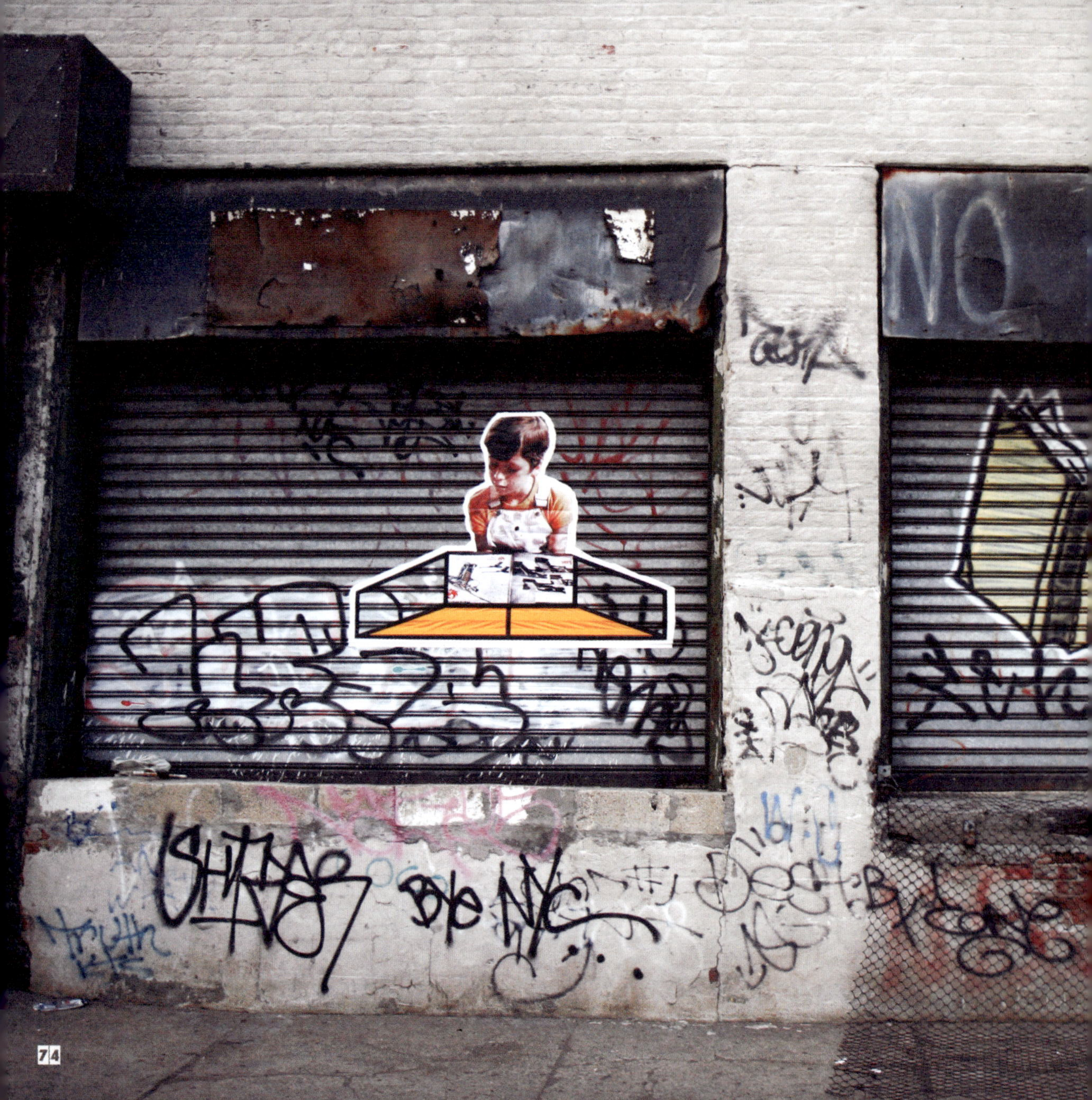
NO

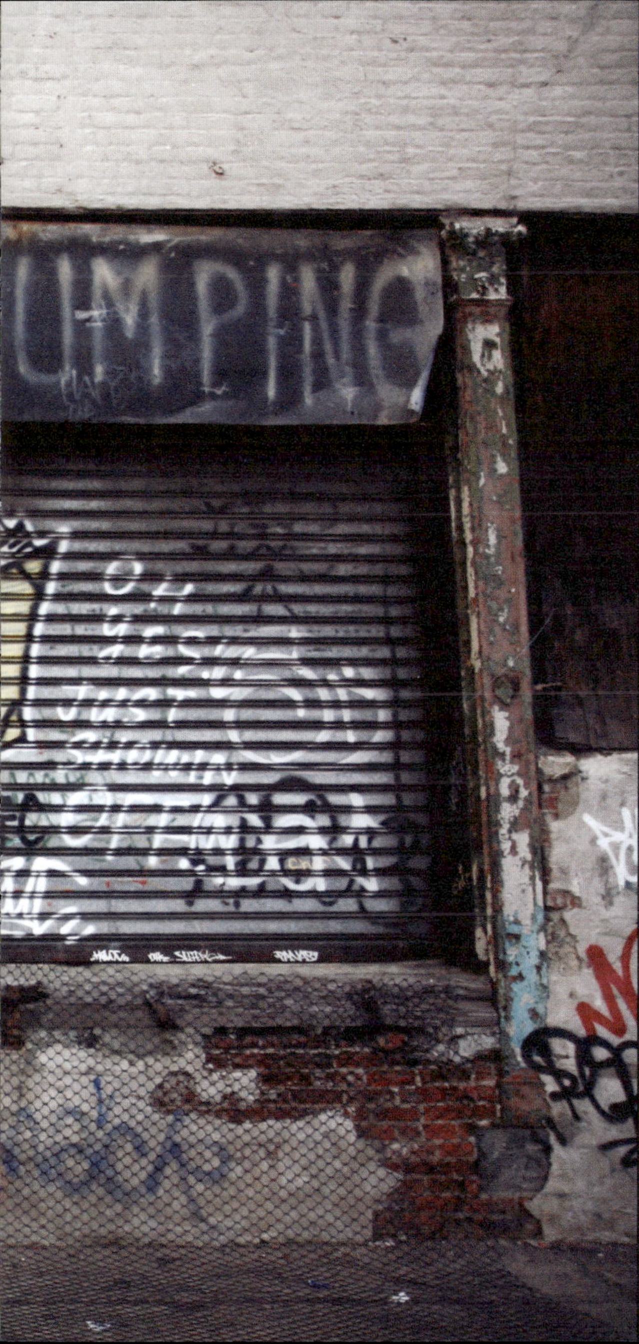

BOOKER TRIBUTE

This collaboration with Aakash Nihalani is a tribute to graffiti artist Booker, inspired by a William Eggleston photograph used in a Whitney ad.

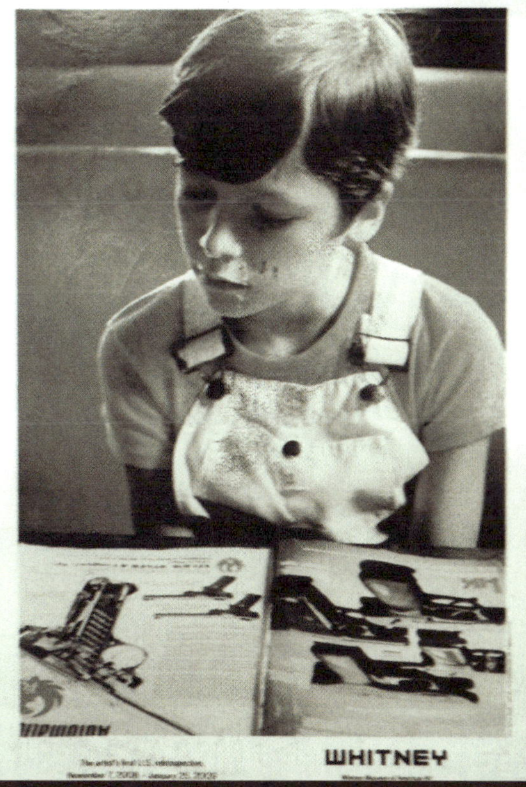

TRICE TRIBUTE

Love it or hate it "shitty" tags are a staple of Brooklyn's landscape.

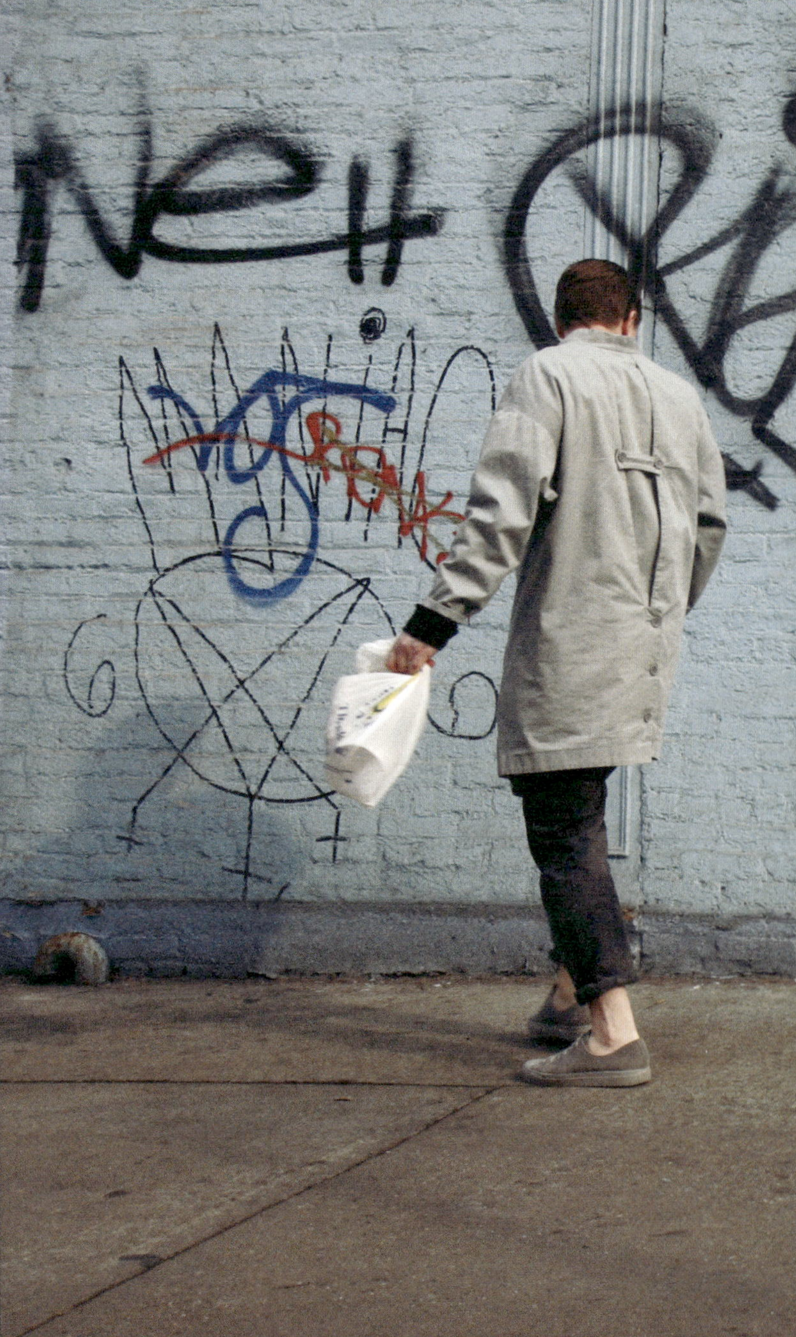

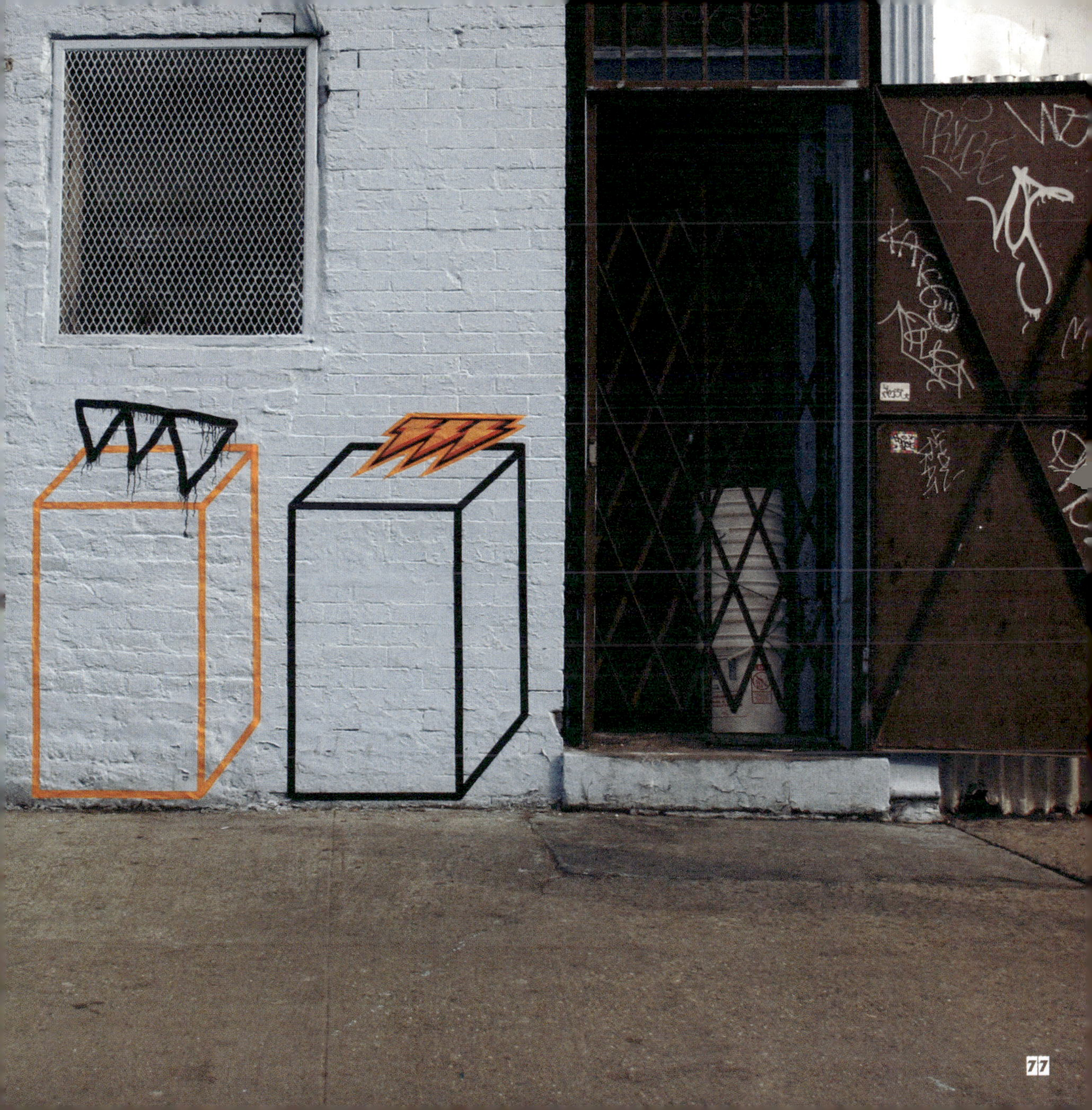

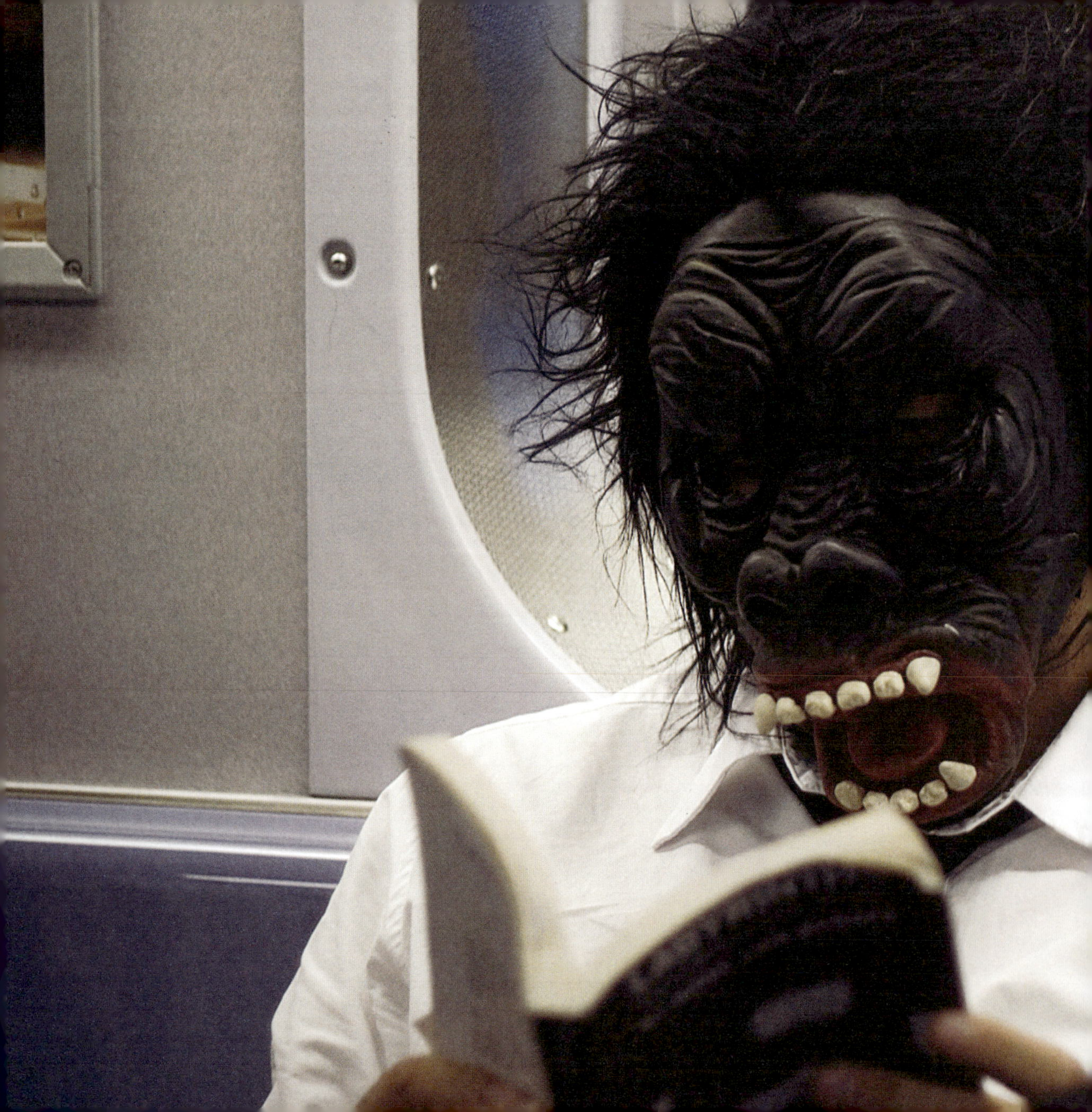

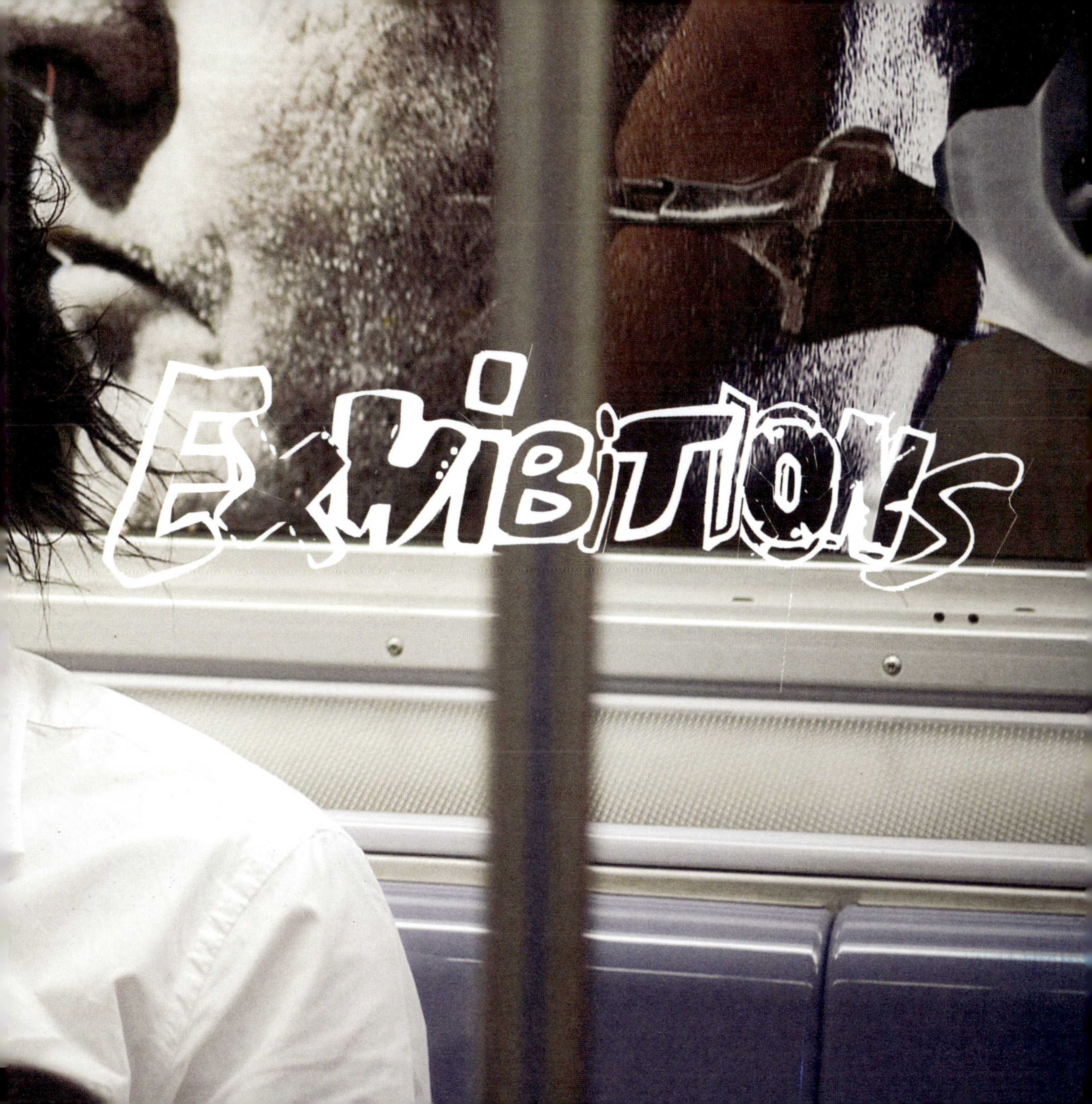
EXHIBITIONS

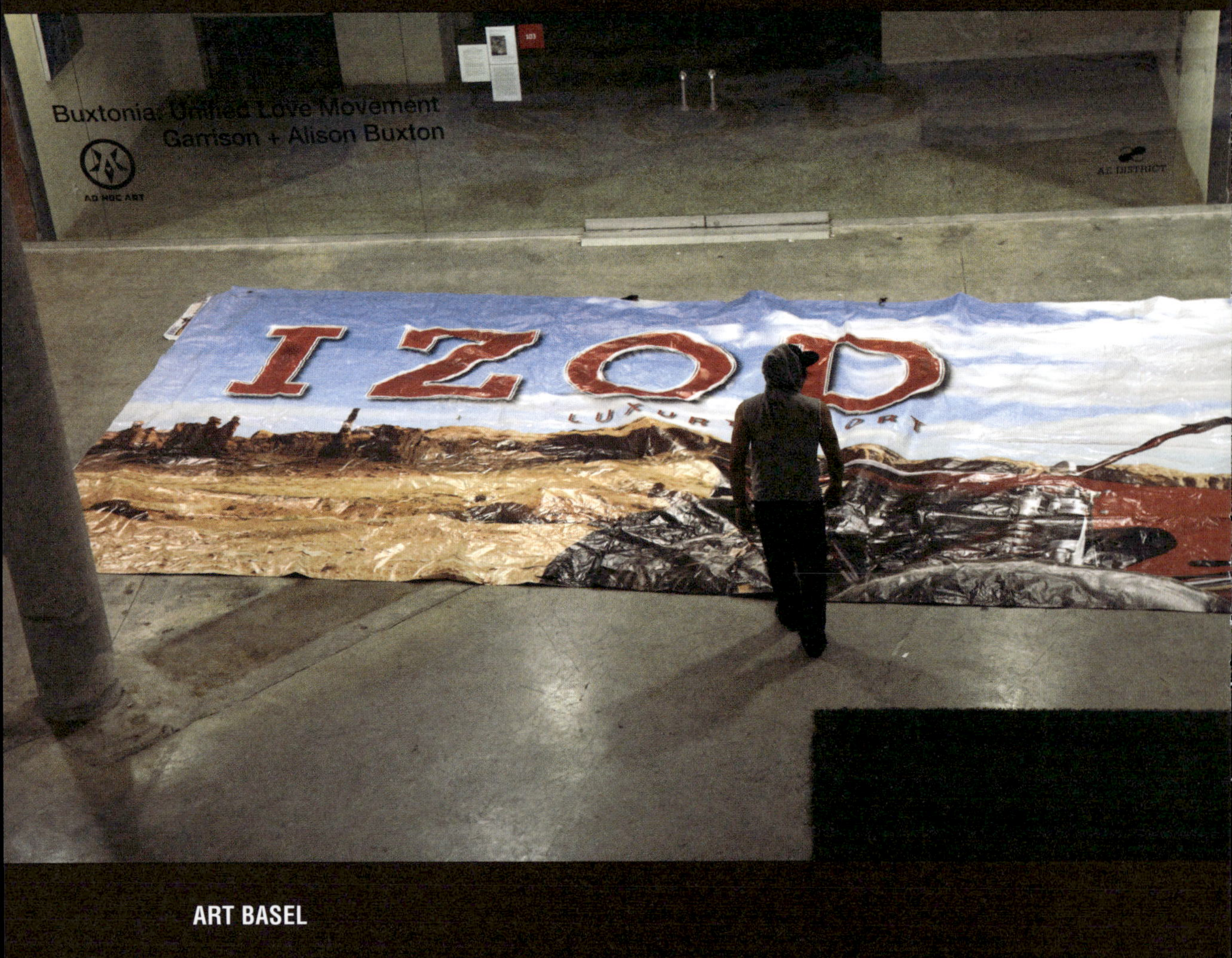
Buxtonia: Unified Love Movement
Garrison + Alison Buxton
AD HOC ART
IZOD

ART BASEL

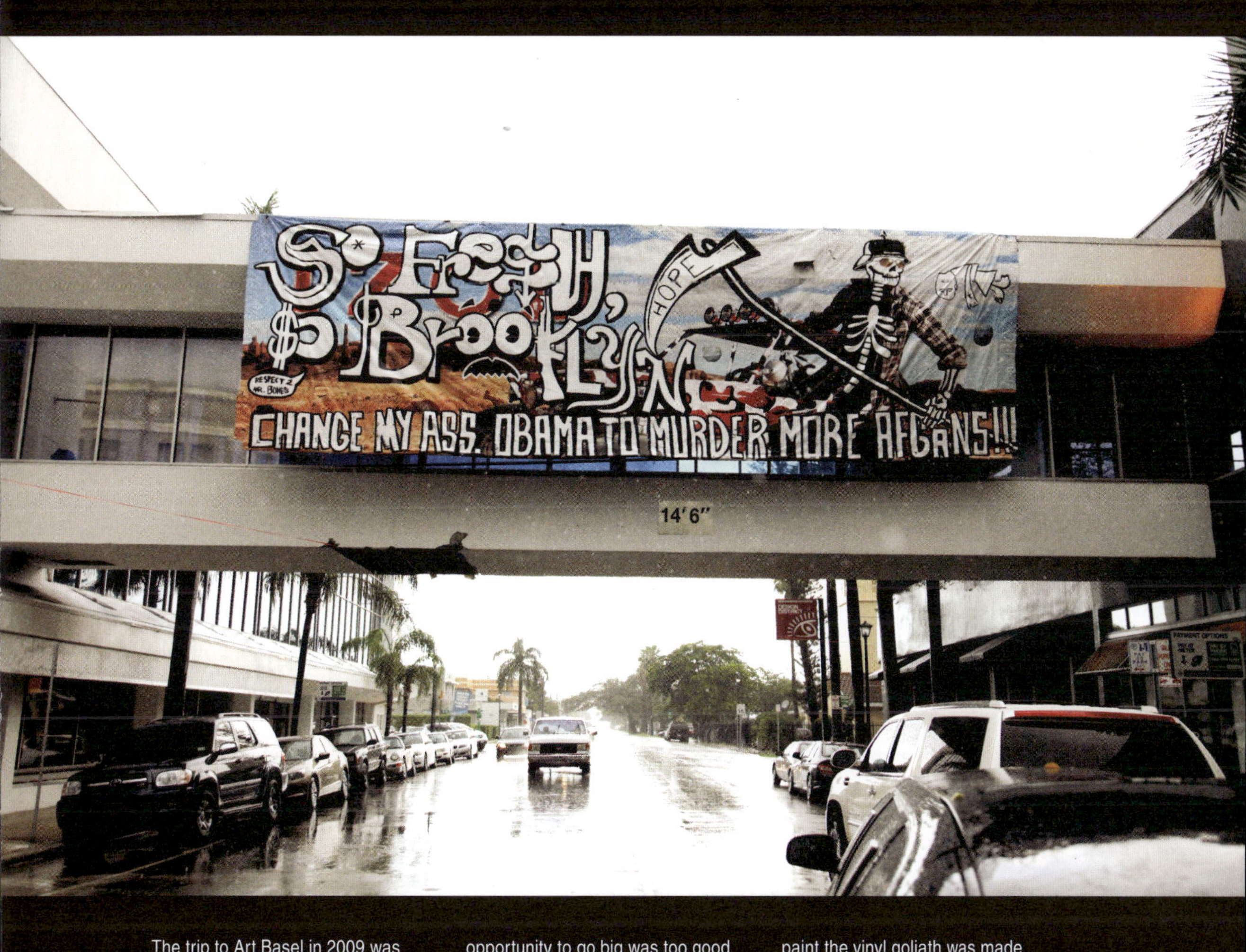

The trip to Art Basel in 2009 was originally about curating and promoting some New York City artists. But, upon arrival it was clear that the opportunity to go big was too good to pass up. The 40-foot billboard was re-installed over one of Art Basel's main roads. With some black & white paint the vinyl goliath was made in the fashion of graffiti king, Mr. Bones—respect.

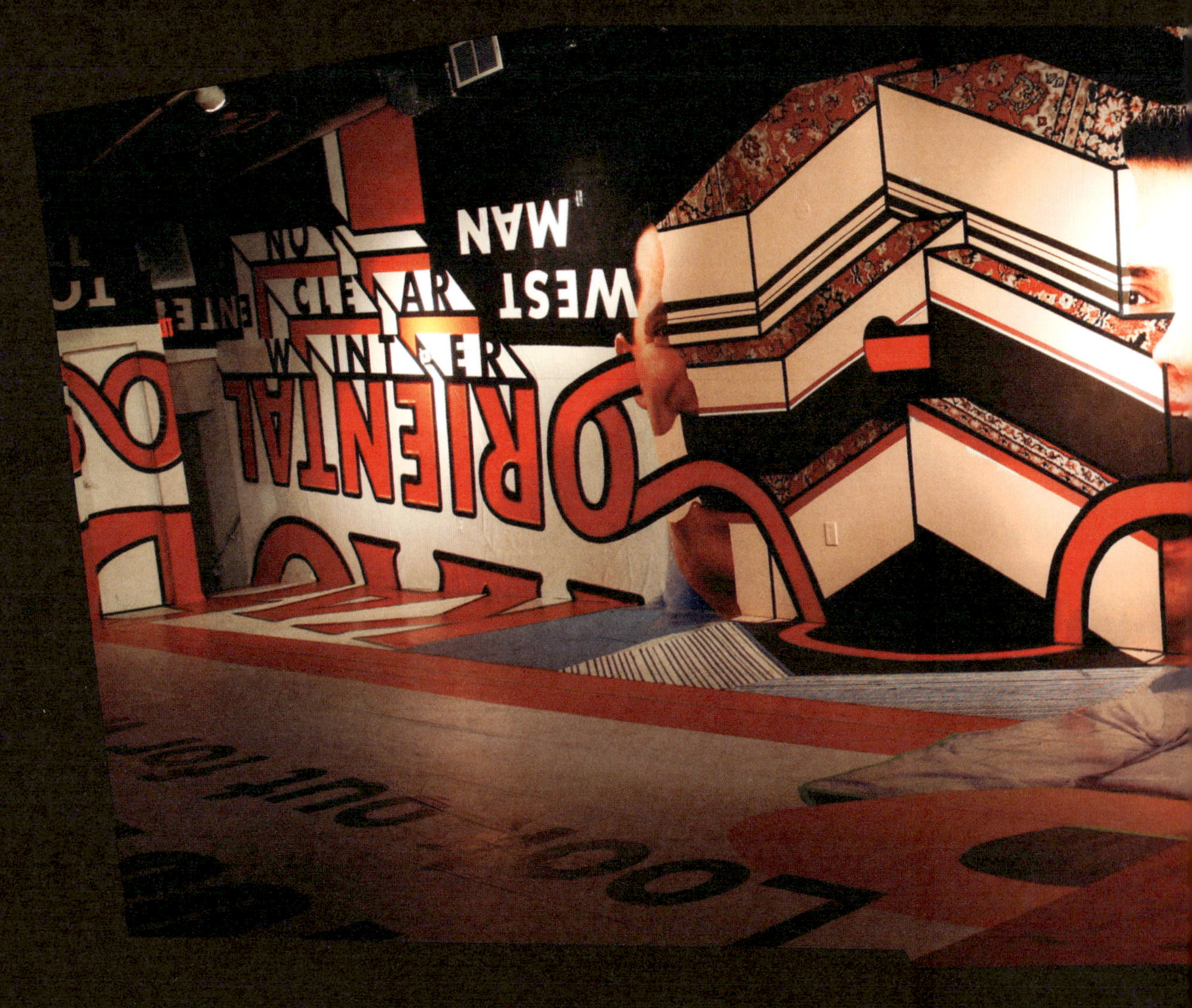

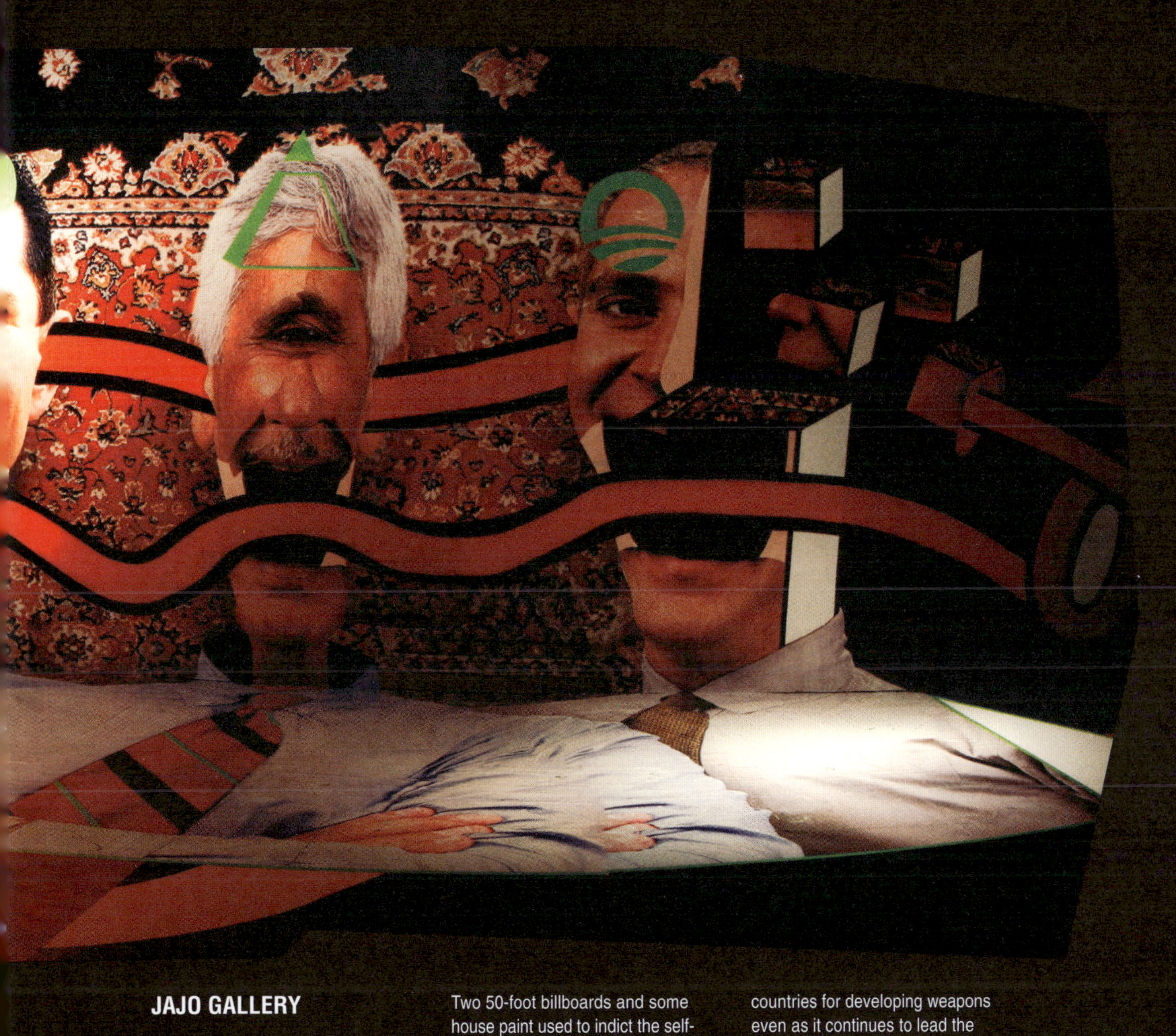

JAJO GALLERY

Two 50-foot billboards and some house paint used to indict the self-proclaimed sheriff of the world. The United States condemns certain countries for developing weapons even as it continues to lead the world in the proliferation of fear.

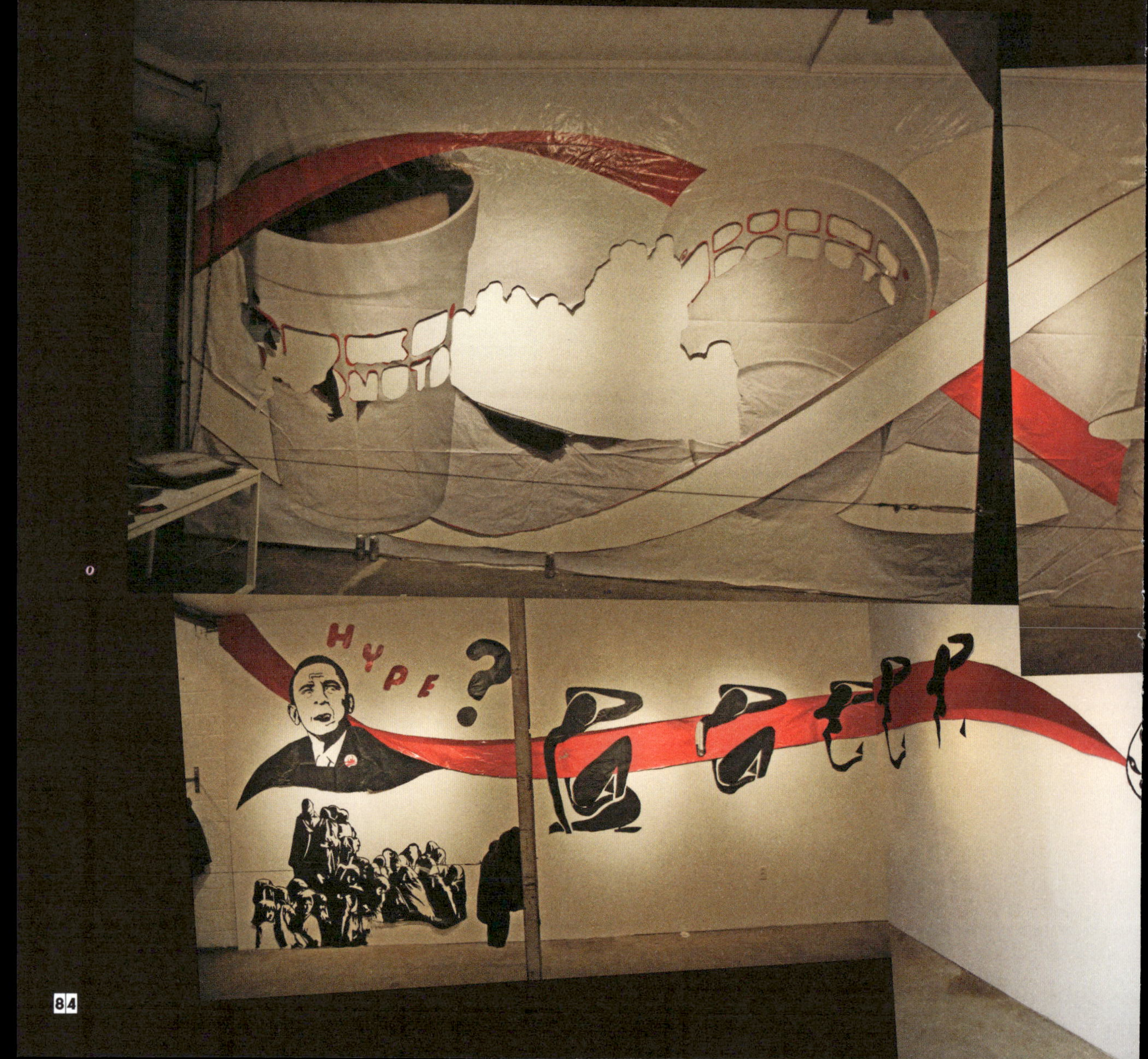
HYPE?

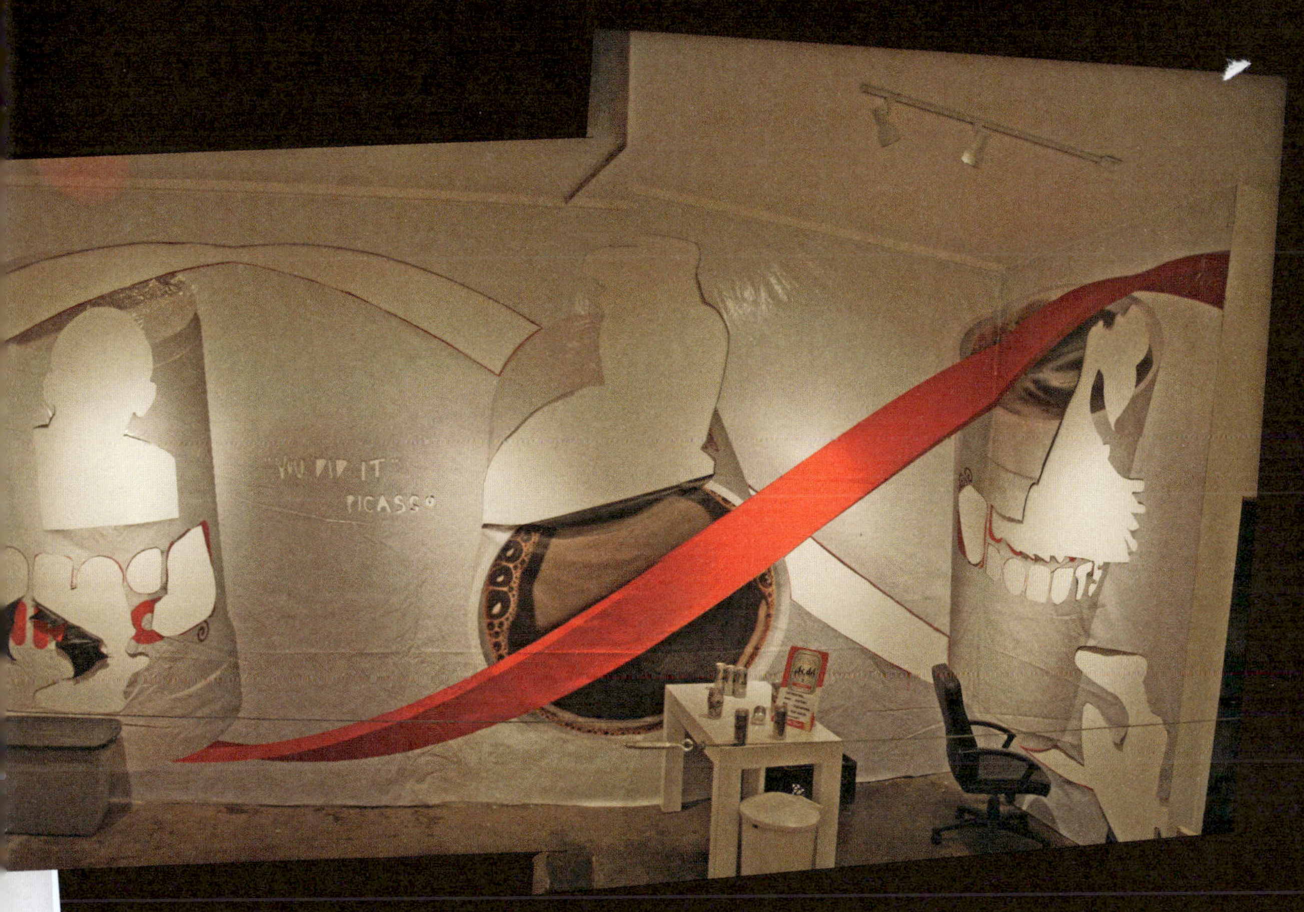

EASTERN DISTRICT

If one street artist could help a president get elected than surely another could help shed light on the truth. However new at the time, the Obama administration was already en route to start where Bush left off. This solo show was meant to mimic the quick slash 'n' paste style from the subway. Without a sketch or plan this 50 foor billboard was mounted and repurposed 24 hours before the doors opened. Shepard Fairey's famous portrait was subverted for this purpose. Picasso and Matisse's famous depictions of women were also used to emphasize the fact that women and children are always the biggest victims of war.

It's the Museum of Modern Art, not contemporary art. For this reason the mash-ups were condemned by MoMA, although MoMA and Happy Corp were fully aware of who was being commissioned to rework the ads. They expected Poster Boy to play nice, but MoMA failed to mention how their "station domination" littered Brooklyn's Atlantic Pacific subway stop with more advertising for its new membership price than anything else. The museum claims it was a selfless promotion of culture. They wouldn't know culture if it came up and slashed their face.

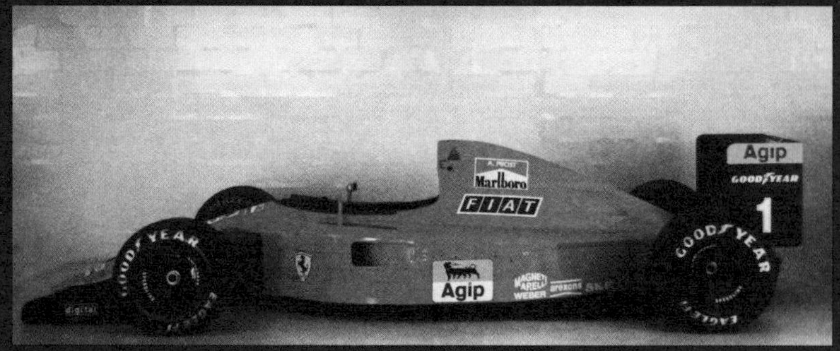

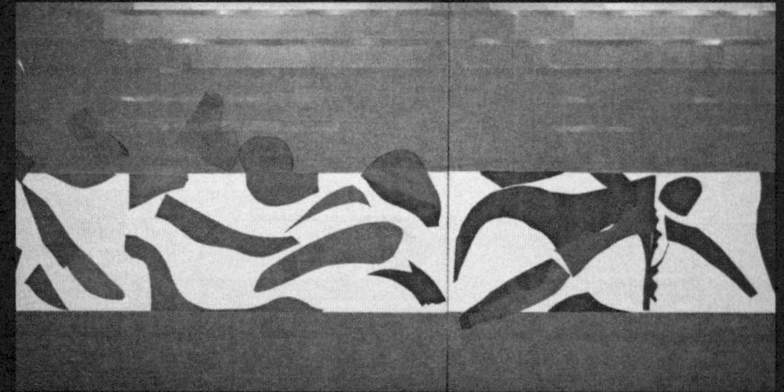

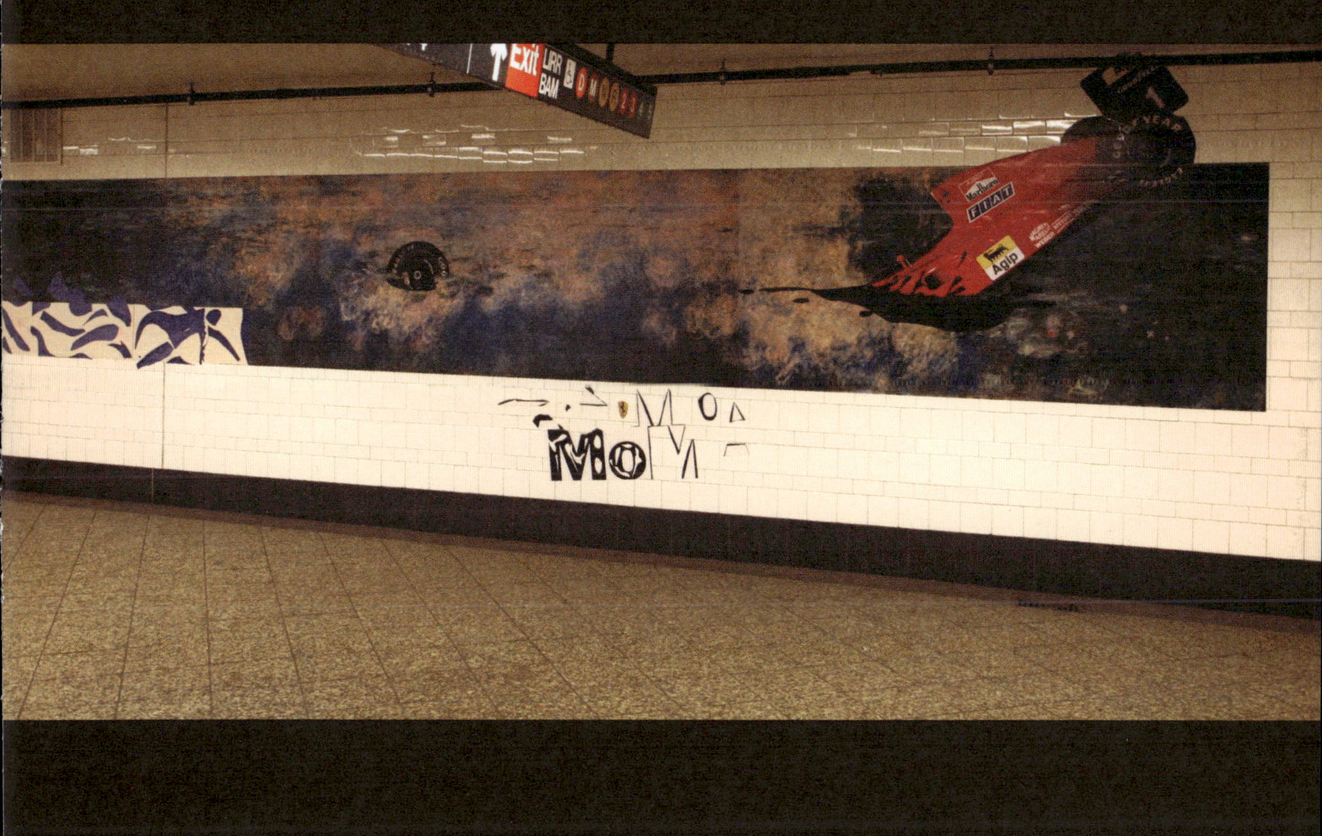

OIL SLICK

The slick veneer of this Monet ad was penetrated by John Bernand's Formula One car while Matisse's swimmers drown in this dangerous metaphor.

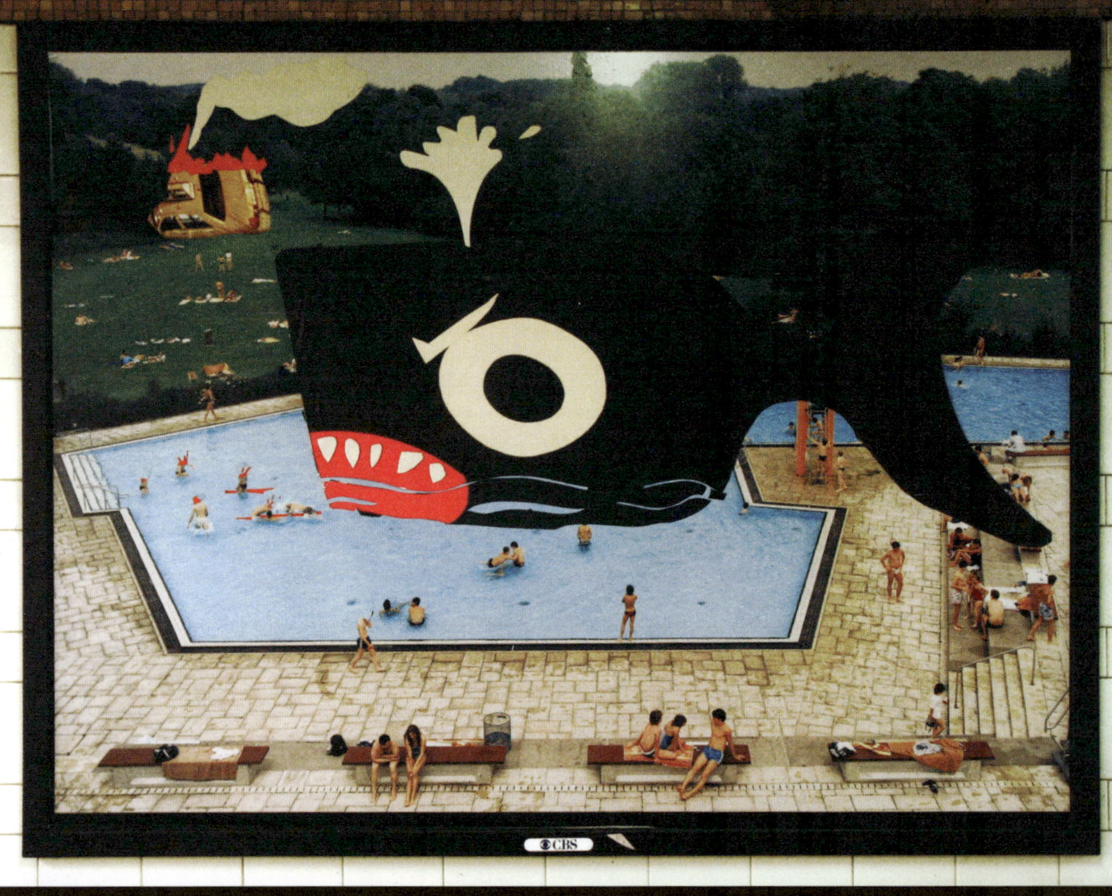

BOTTLED IN / GONE FISH'

Arp's "Navel Bottle" sits uncomfortably well in Gursky's swimming pool.

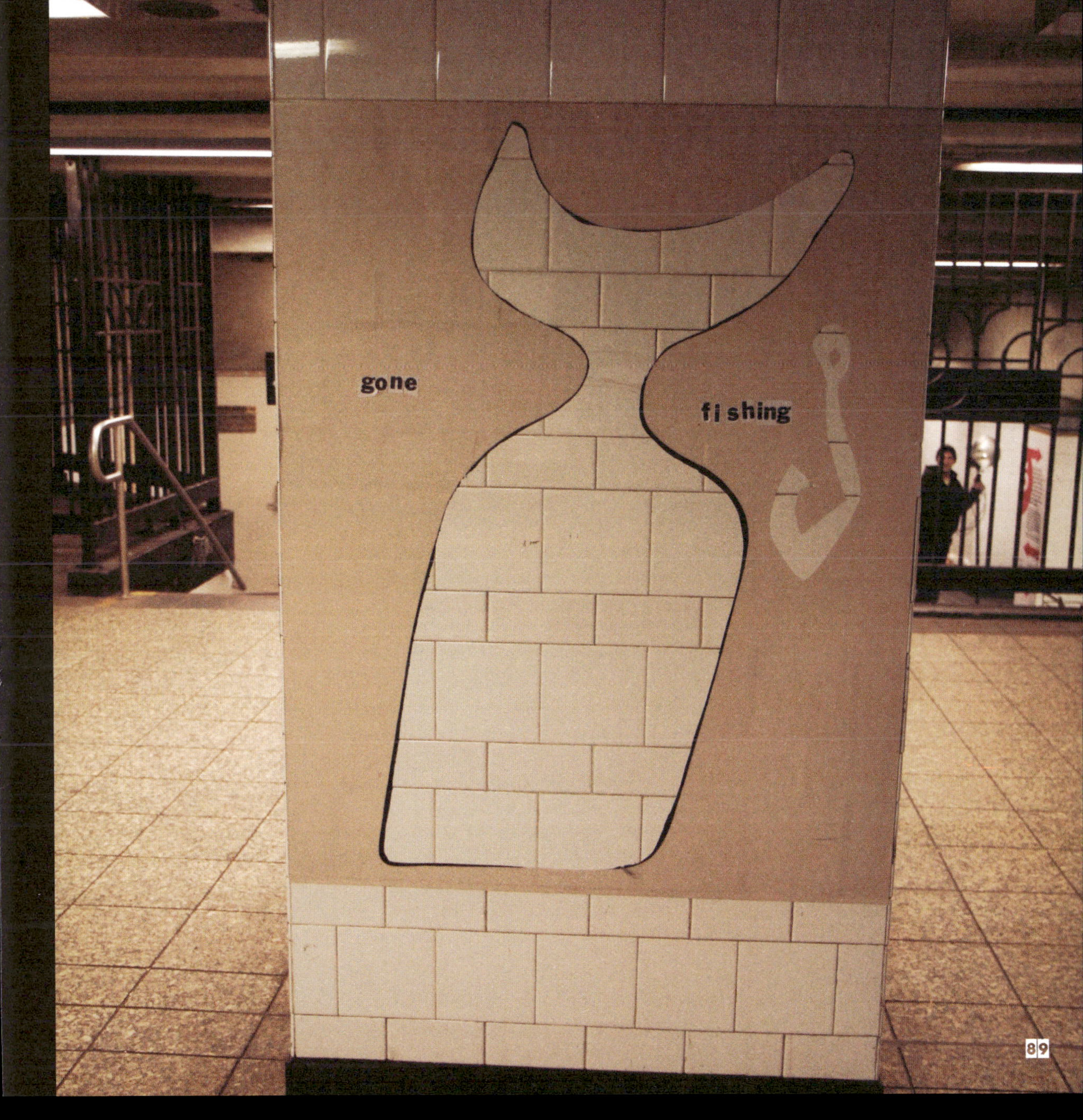
gone
fishing

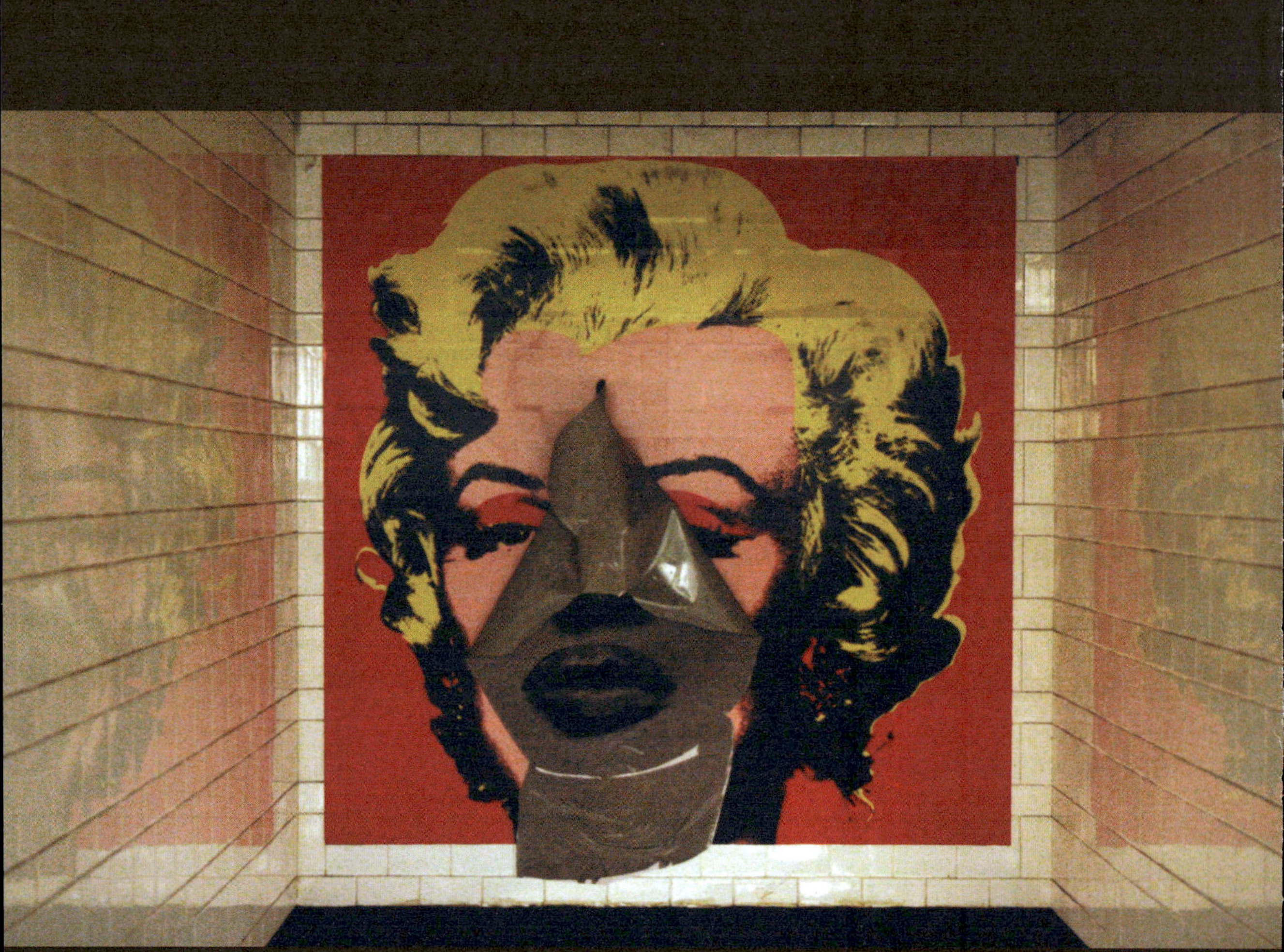

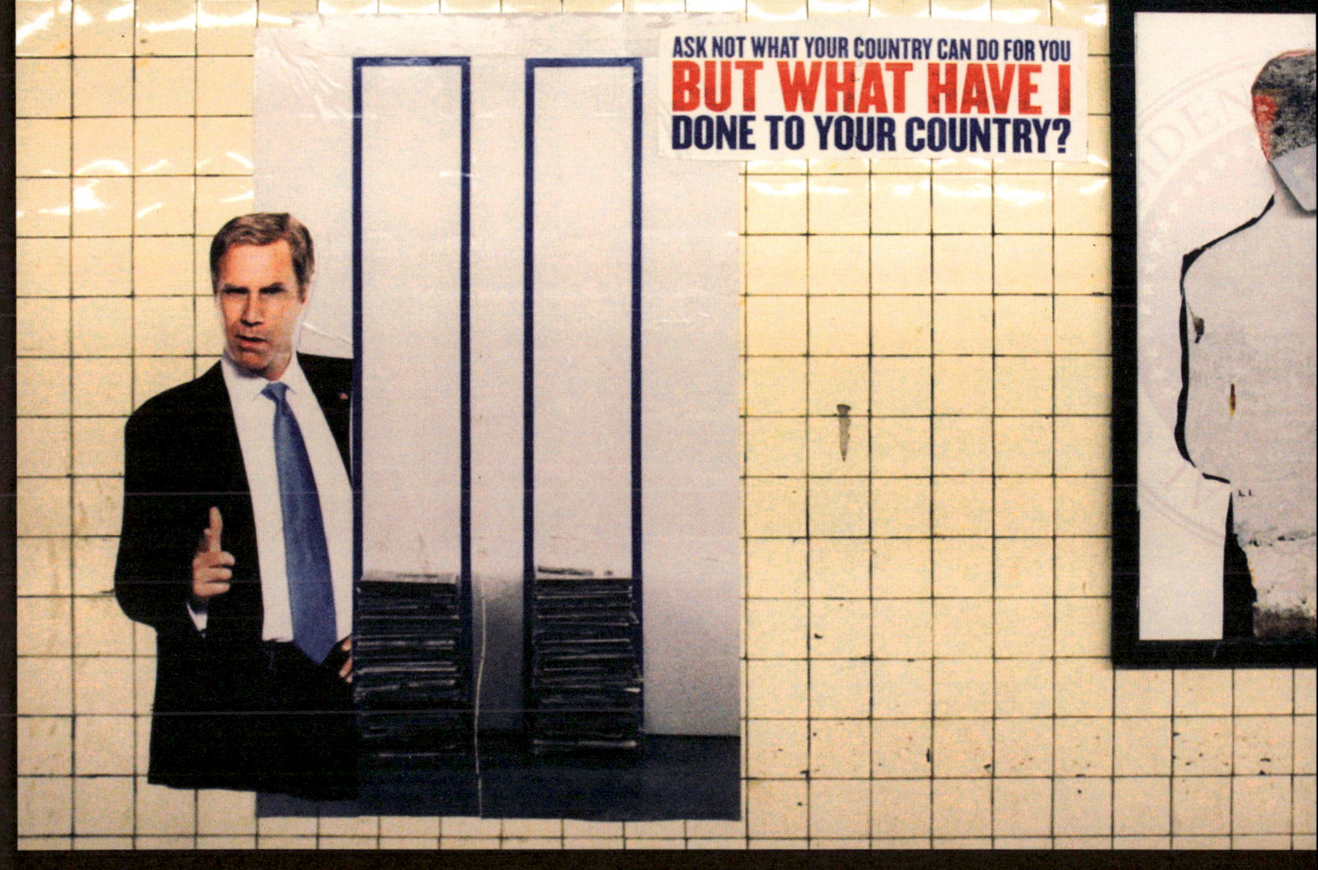

WHAT IS BEEF?

The title is taken from a Blackstar (Mos Def & Talib Kweli) track. As Mos Def spits it: "Beef is not what these famous niggas do on the mic. Beef is what George Bush would do in a fight."

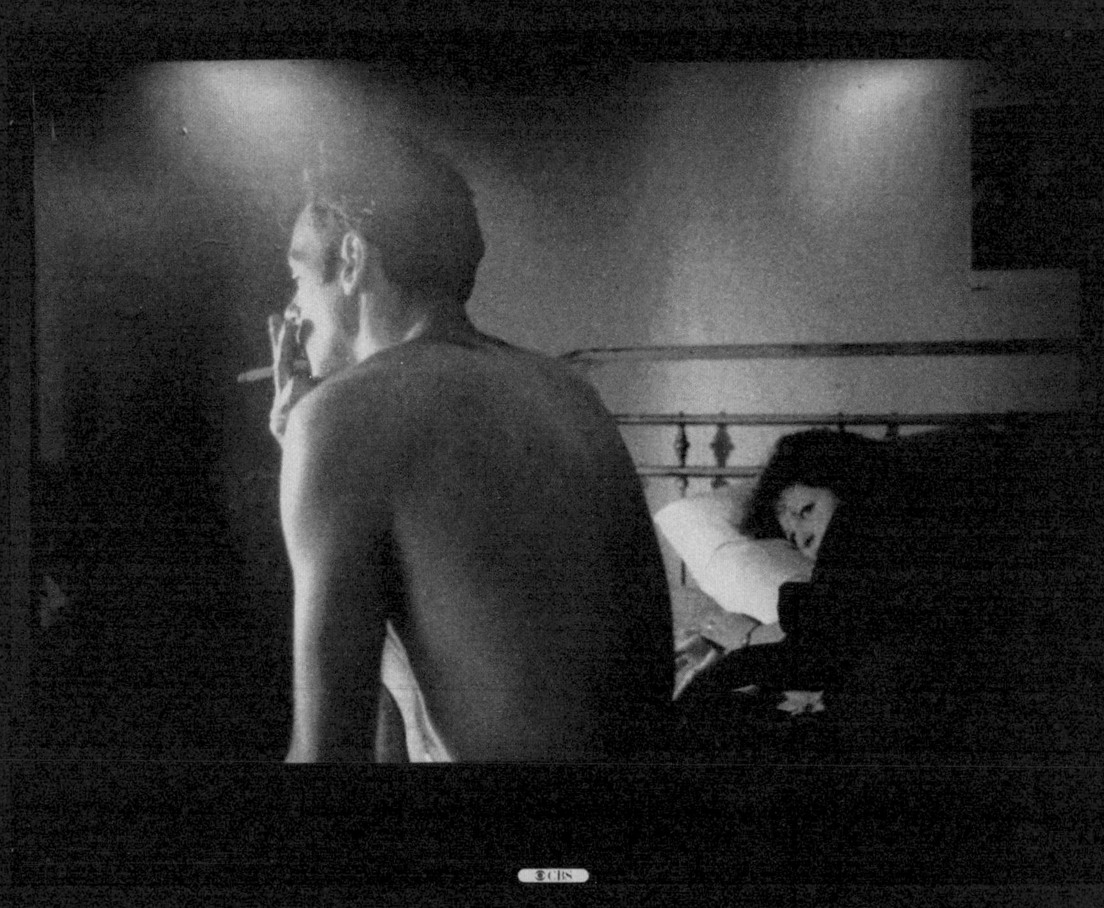

W.I.L.M.A.

It stands for: "Wallpaper Isn't Lesser Modern Art." The drawn-out acronym definitely came after the piece was completed, but the inspiration was instantaneous. Everyone knows Nan Goldin's "Nan and Brian in Bed." But, most people don't notice the photo of Brian and Fred Flintstone in the top

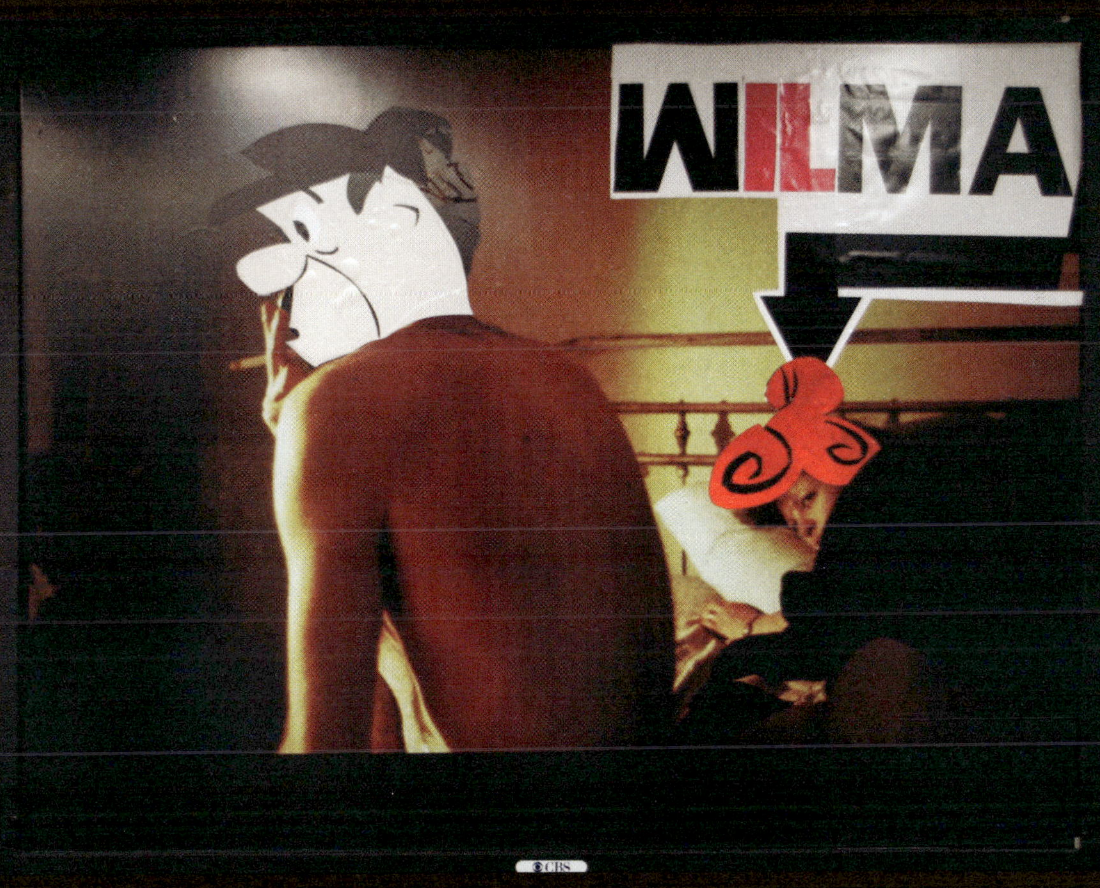

right-hand corner of the famous photo. This overlooked detail prompted the freehand portrait of Mr. Flintstone from his cigarette commercial days.

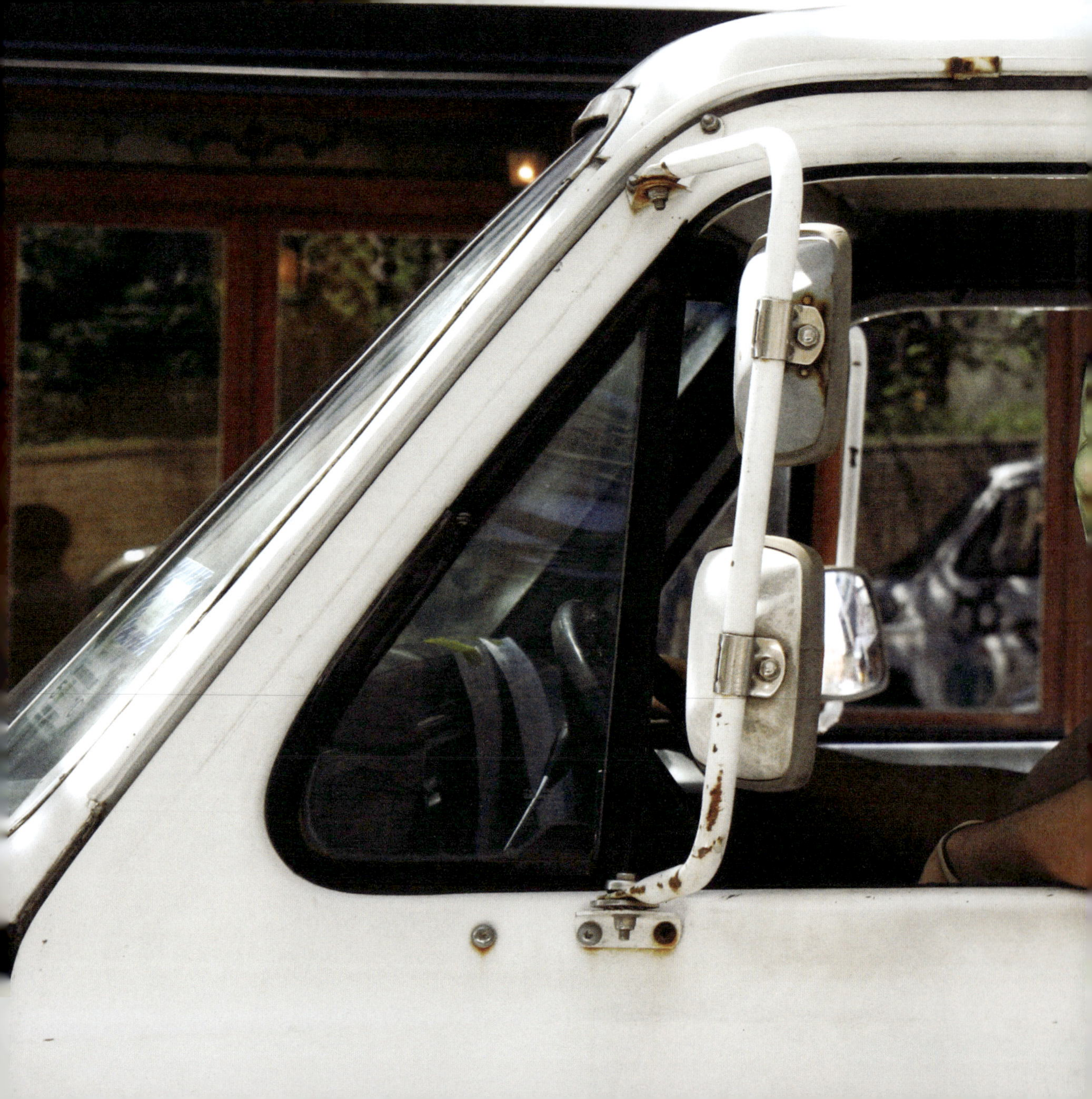

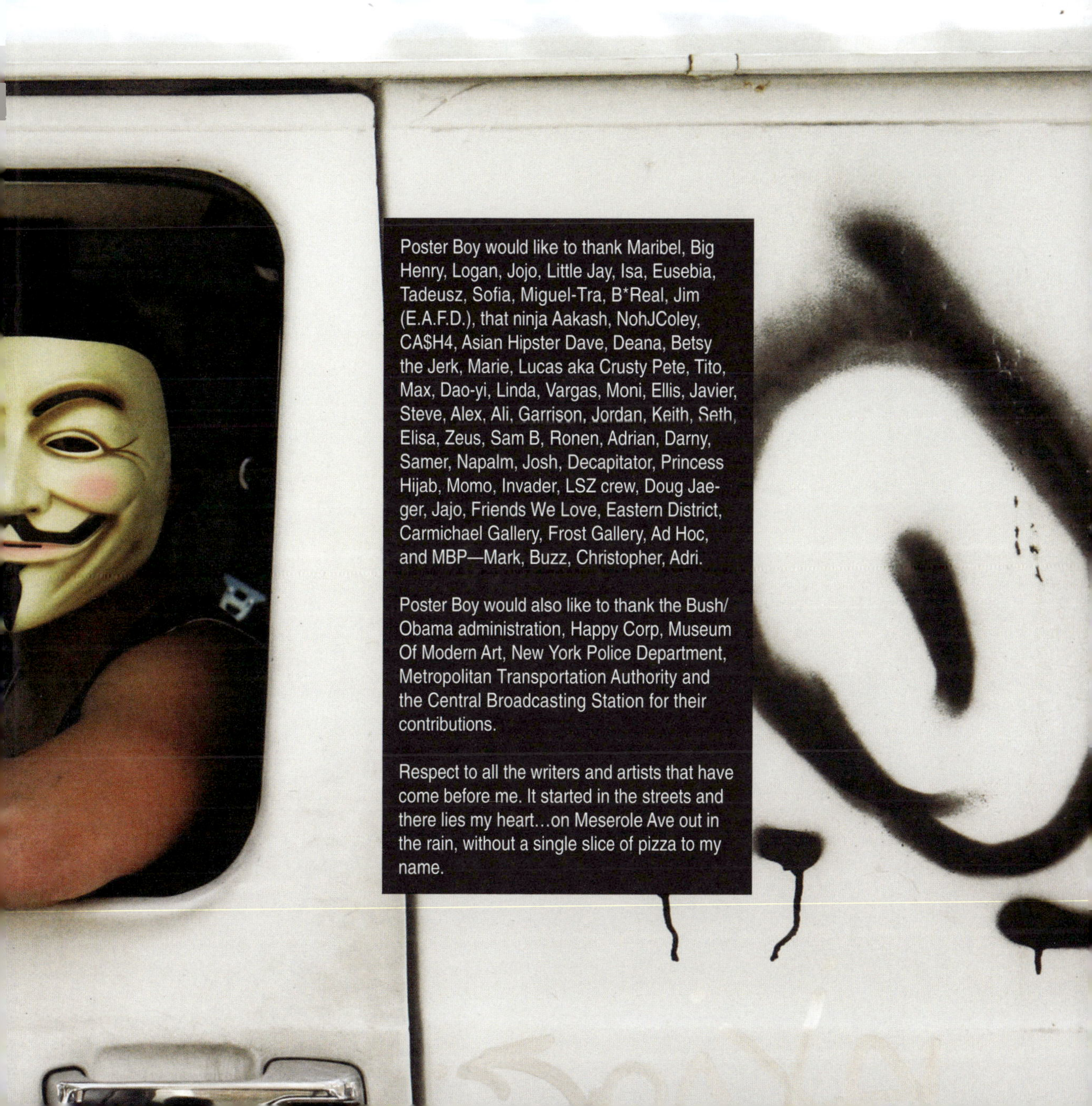

Poster Boy would like to thank Maribel, Big Henry, Logan, Jojo, Little Jay, Isa, Eusebia, Tadeusz, Sofia, Miguel-Tra, B*Real, Jim (E.A.F.D.), that ninja Aakash, NohJColey, CA$H4, Asian Hipster Dave, Deana, Betsy the Jerk, Marie, Lucas aka Crusty Pete, Tito, Max, Dao-yi, Linda, Vargas, Moni, Ellis, Javier, Steve, Alex, Ali, Garrison, Jordan, Keith, Seth, Elisa, Zeus, Sam B, Ronen, Adrian, Darny, Samer, Napalm, Josh, Decapitator, Princess Hijab, Momo, Invader, LSZ crew, Doug Jaeger, Jajo, Friends We Love, Eastern District, Carmichael Gallery, Frost Gallery, Ad Hoc, and MBP—Mark, Buzz, Christopher, Adri.

Poster Boy would also like to thank the Bush/Obama administration, Happy Corp, Museum Of Modern Art, New York Police Department, Metropolitan Transportation Authority and the Central Broadcasting Station for their contributions.

Respect to all the writers and artists that have come before me. It started in the streets and there lies my heart…on Meserole Ave out in the rain, without a single slice of pizza to my name.

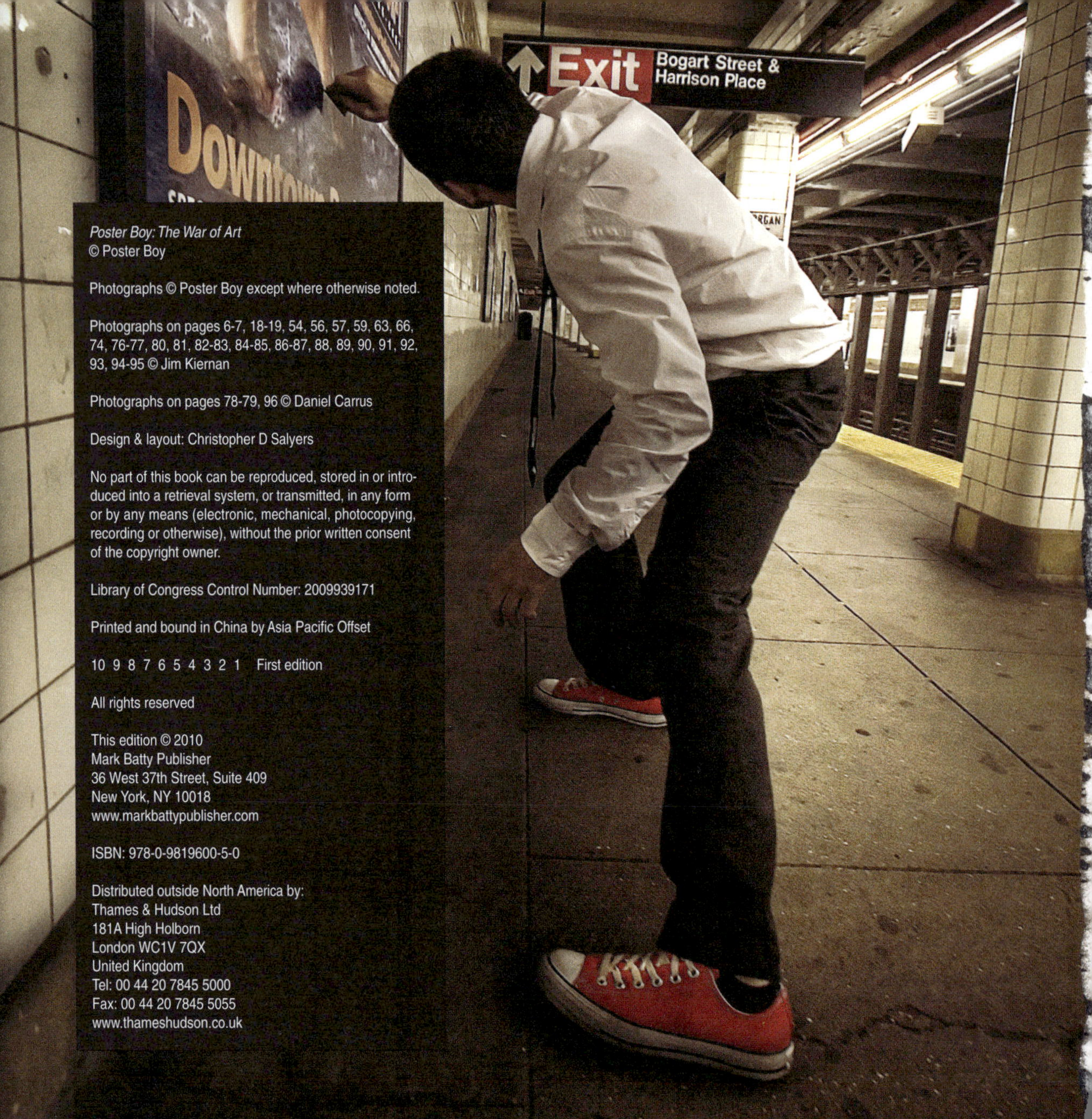

Poster Boy: The War of Art

Design & layout: Christopher D Salyers

Library of Congress Control Number: 2009939171

Printed and bound in China by Asia Pacific Offset

10 9 8 7 6 5 4 3 2 1 First edition

Mark Batty Publisher
36 West 37th Street, Suite 409
New York, NY 10018
www.markbattypublisher.com

ISBN: 978-0-9819600-5-0

Distributed outside North America by:
Thames & Hudson Ltd
181A High Holborn
London WC1V 7QX
United Kingdom
Tel: 00 44 20 7845 5000
Fax: 00 44 20 7845 5055
www.thameshudson.co.uk

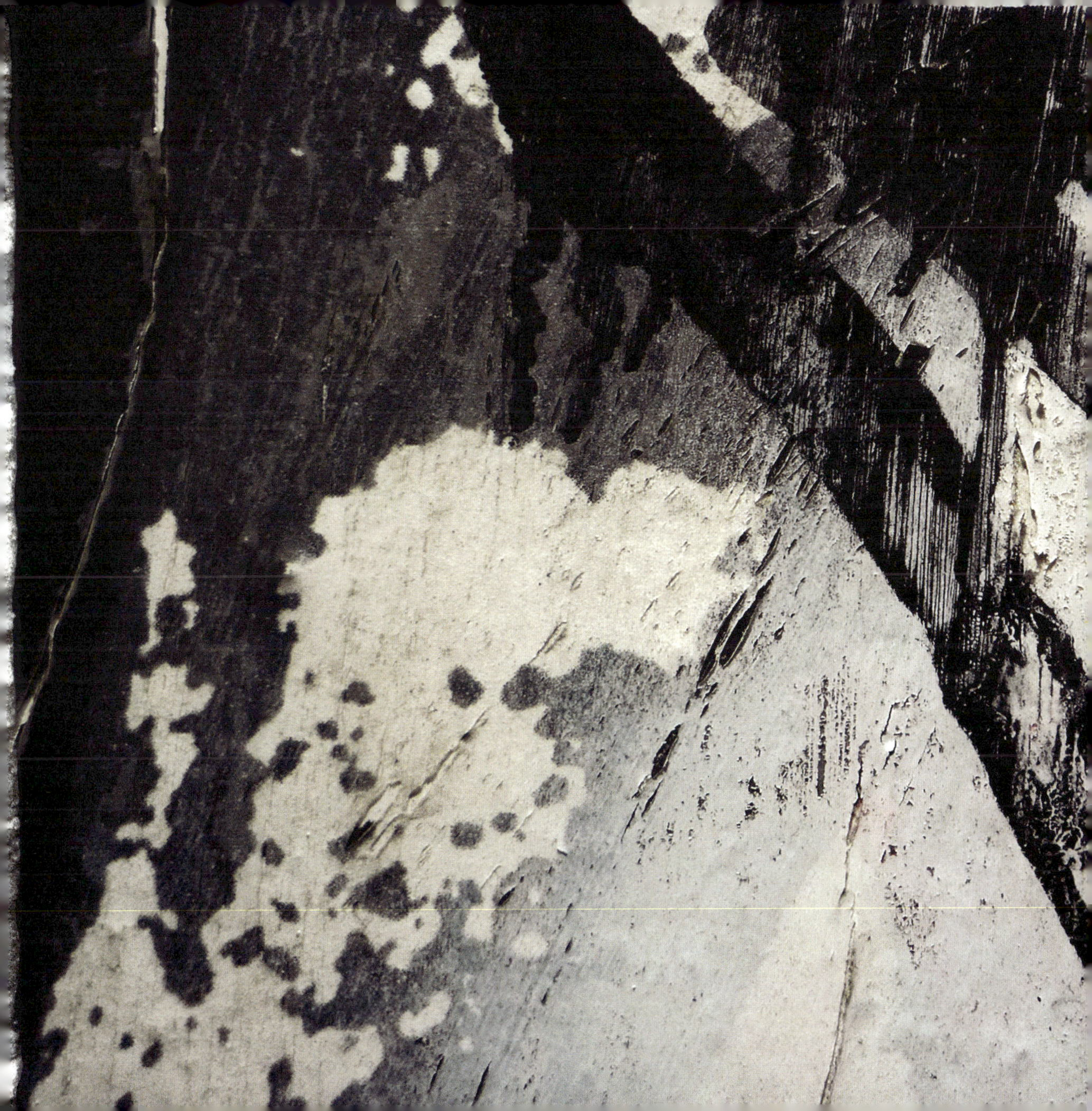

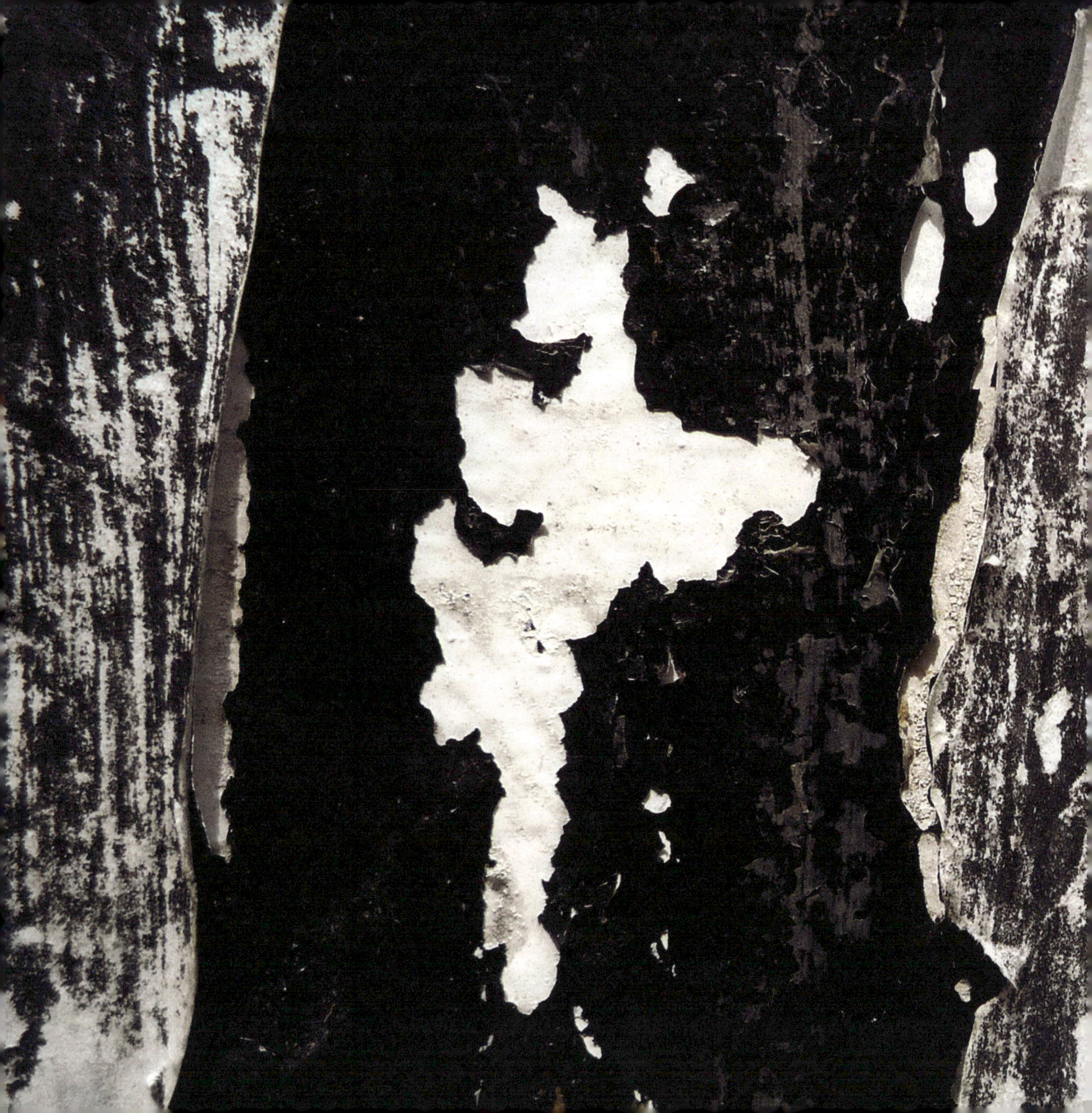